The Information Capital

LONDON
The Information Capital

100 maps and graphics that will change how you view the city

James Cheshire

Oliver Uberti

**PARTICULAR
BOOKS**
an imprint of
PENGUIN BOOKS

PARTICULAR BOOKS

Published by the Penguin Group
Penguin Books Ltd, 80 Strand, London WC2R 0RL, England
Penguin Group (USA) Inc., 375 Hudson Street, New York, New York 10014, USA
Penguin Group (Canada), 90 Eglinton Avenue East, Suite 700, Toronto, Ontario, Canada M4P 2Y3 (a division of Pearson Penguin Canada Inc.)
Penguin Ireland, 25 St Stephen's Green, Dublin 2, Ireland (a division of Penguin Books Ltd)
Penguin Group (Australia), 707 Collins Street, Melbourne, Victoria 3008, Australia (a division of Pearson Australia Group Pty Ltd)
Penguin Books India Pvt Ltd, 11 Community Centre, Panchsheel Park, New Delhi – 110 017, India
Penguin Group (NZ), 67 Apollo Drive, Rosedale, North Shore 0632, New Zealand (a division of Pearson New Zealand Ltd)
Penguin Books (South Africa) (Pty) Ltd, Block D, Rosebank Office Park, 181 Jan Smuts Avenue, Parktown North, Gauteng 2193, South Africa

Penguin Books Ltd, Registered Offices: 80 Strand, London WC2R 0RL, England

www.penguin.com

First published in Great Britain by Particular Books 2014
2

Copyright © James Cheshire and Oliver Uberti, 2014

The moral right of the authors has been asserted

Designed by Oliver Uberti
Set in Whitney (Hoefler & Co.) with a cameo by London's own Founder's Caslon (ITC)
Printed and bound in Italy by Graphicom srl

A CIP catalogue record for this book is available from the British Library

978-1-846-14847-7

JAMES
to Isla and my parents

OLIVER
for my parents, who were married in London

Contents

THE GRAPHICS

Where We Are

36 CONTOURS OF THE CITY

38 CITY OF VILLAGES

40 HUB FOR THE WORLD

44 DAY AND NIGHT

46 HOT SPOTS

48 SEEKING SHADE

52 HOLDING BACK THE TIDE

54 IF THESE STREETS COULD TALK

56 WHAT LIES BENEATH

60 WEST LONDON: 120 YEARS LATER

62 BACK FROM THE BLITZ

64 GENERATION RENT

68 13 VIEWS WORTH PROTECTING

Who We Are

76 DNA OF THE CITY

78 THE POPULATION REBOUND

86 PROFESSIONAL NETWORKING

88 THERE'S A GUILD FOR THAT

90 FIFTY KILOMETRES OF JOBS

98 PASSPORTS, PLEASE

100 ETHNICITY

102 COUNTING THE INVISIBLE

Where We Go

112 TWITTER TRIPS

114 TUBE FLOWS

124 GETTING TO WORK

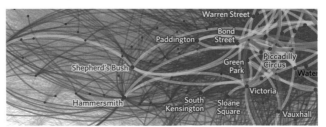

126 TO AND FRO, ON THE TUBE

128 A WEEK ON THE UNDERGROUND

80 SIMILARITIES ATTRACT

82 LIFE AND DEATH

Cohabiting

Married

Single

Single

84 RELATIONSHIP STATUS

HARINGEY

WALTHAM FOREST

BRENT

CAMDEN

ISLINGTON

HACKNEY

92 THE COLOUR OF VOTES

9,800

12,600

21,600

38,900

West Midlands   South West   East of England   South East

London

9,300

94 MOVING IN, THEN ON

Lithuania +37,500

Romania +41,800

Nepal +17,600

Bulgaria +24,200

Slovakia +10,600

96 INCREASINGLY EASTERN

104 GREETINGS FROM LONDON

106 TWITTER INK

108 WHO LONDON INSPIRED

116 UNTANGLED ON ARRIVAL

120 THAMES GATEWAY

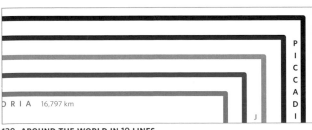

PICCADI

ORIA   16,797 km

130 AROUND THE WORLD IN 10 LINES

132 DISRUPTED

134 THE TUBE CHALLENGE

136 ROUTE MASTERS

138 MENTAL MAPS

148 BORIS'S BEST BIKERS

150 EXHAUSTING RIDES

152 CABLE CAR TO NOWHERE

How We're Doing

162 ISLINGTON HAS ISSUES

164 A TALE OF TWO CITIES

172 CAUSES OF DEATH

174 QUIT RATES

176 PILL BOXES

184 YOU CAN'T HIDE

186 SOUND THE ALARM!

188 SAFER DRIVERS

142 MINICAB CORRIDORS

144 LOST & FOUND

146 THE MORNING RIDE

154 RUN!

158 WHY NOT WALK IT?

166 LIVES ON THE LINE

168 WHAT'S TO EAT?

170 THE SHAPE OF OBESITY

178 CALL 999

180 FLASHPOINTS

182 TOP CRIMES

190 HOW CYCLISTS GET HIT

192 STREET VIEWS

194 THE UNCONNECTED

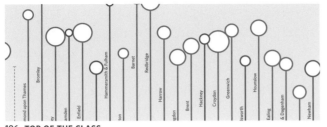

196 TOP OF THE CLASS

FRIEND — ENEMY
CHICKEN — EGG
DRAGON — SNAKE
CAT — DOG
ZOMBIE — VAMPIRE

198 IN THEIR WORDS

What We Like

210 A TRUE ZOO

74
51
Sir Sidney Nolan 135
Leon Ferrari 199
92
Robert Motherwell
Sir Terry Frost
Patrick Heron
Joseph Beuys 578
Richard Hamilton 138
Diane Arbus 69
Leon Kossoff 116
Andy Warhol 272
Joe Tilson 152

212 ALL THE TATE'S TREASURES

214 FOLLOWING THE LEADER

222 WHO SAYS PRINT IS DEAD?

Arts architecture, art, poetry

Transport TfL, Tube, trains
Tube strike

224 THE BUZZ ABOUT TOWN

54,000
MEN seeking WOMEN
NARROWEST 10 years

70,000
WOMEN seeking MEN
NARROWEST 10 years

226 LOOKING FOR LOVE

202 **THE FOOTBALL TRIBES**

204 **THINGS TO DO**

206 **PHOTOGENIC FEATURES**

216 **FASHION CYCLES**

218 **THEY CAME, THEY SAW, THEY SPENT**

220 **SHOP WINDOW**

228 **HAPPY TIMES**

232 **BOOKS, COFFEE, ETC.**

Acknowledgements

Without those working tirelessly with London's data in its universities, museums, businesses and local government, London would not be 'The Information Capital'. We are tremendously fortunate to have received the support and expertise from some of the best through their data, graphics and advice. This book would not have been possible without them.

When it comes to mapping 21st-century London, Oliver O'Brien is unsurpassed. We are extremely grateful to him for being part of this project from the start. His data, expertise, fact-checking and much welcome feedback have been integral to ensuring the graphics here are the best they can be.

We are indebted to those at University College London (UCL) who have been particularly generous with their time and expertise. From the Centre for Advanced Spatial Analysis (CASA) we would like to thank Shlomit Flint for her fascinating insights into one small area of east London; Ed Manley for his 'Tube flows' and 'Minicab Corridors' graphics and his continued support throughout the project; Joan Serras for the bus data used in 'Route Masters'; Hannah Fry for her detailed comments and enthusiasm for our work; Steven Gray, Robin Edwards, Flora Roumpani, Duncan Smith, and Camilo Vargas for their help with data queries. At the UCL Department of Geography, we extend our thanks to Muhammad Adnan, Alistair Leak and Guy Lansley for their Twitter data wizardry; to Matt Disney for wrangling the NDVI satellite imagery; and to Peter Wood for his thorough read-through and helpful feedback. Thanks to Matt Ashby from UCL SECReT for his violent crime graphic and to Anna Mavrogianni and colleagues from the UCL Bartlett Faculty of the Built Environment for their urban heat island research.

At the London School of Hygiene and Tropical Medicine, we would like to thank Daniel Lewis for helpful comments on our drafts and also Anna Goodman for her collaboration on the Boris Bikes data. Thanks to Luke Sibieta and Ellen Greaves from the Institute of Fiscal Studies for their help with our 'Top of the Class' graphic. We are also particularly grateful to the team at City University - Aidan Slingsby, Alexander Kachkaev, Jo Wood and Jason Dykes – for their brilliant Flickr map behind 'Photogenic Features'; to Jon Reades (Kings College London) for his 'Week in the Life of the Underground' graphic; to Kiril Stanilov (University of Cambridge) for his painstakingly digitised historic street and land use data; to Alex Singleton (University of Liverpool) for the London Output Area Classification; and to George MacKerron (University of Sussex) for the 'Happy Times' graphic. Thanks also to André Bruggmann (University of Zurich) for his help with the network analysis and the word frequency counts required on a number of graphics and to Jack Harrison (Ordnance Survey) for his work gathering the road accident data.

We extend our gratitude to Adam Towle of the Greater London Authority and Cass Cities for not only sporting the red laces in the Introduction, but also for his help and enthusiasm on a number of graphics in this book, not least the map of London's localities he created. Thanks also to ultimate Londoner, Matt Brown, for the (mostly true) ghost stories and for sharing tag data from Londonist. We would also like to thank Ken Titmuss for his stories in 'If These Streets Could Talk'. We are also grateful to Jay Carver, Marit Leenstra and Rose Malik at Crossrail for granting us access to their finds for 'What Lies Beneath'. Thank you to Ben Payne, Alistair Hall and the great people at Ministry of Stories for sharing their words with us; to EDITD and Francesco Franchi for sharing their fashion wheels and Ferris wheels; and to Malcolm Linskey of Taxi Trade Promotions for sharing his 'Knowledge'. Thanks to Neil Stewart for providing the Booth Map from the LSE Library and Christopher Fleet at the National Library of Scotland for the 19th Century Ordnance Survey Map. We are grateful to Gareth Rees and Louise Crow at MySociety for providing the Freedom of Information data from *whatdotheyknow. com*; Fiona Scott for providing data and comments for our 'Fifty Kilometres of Jobs' graphic and Julian Harrap Architects LLP for use of their photo collage; Fredrik Lindahl at FlightRadar24 for the allowing us to use the flight track data; Anke and Lars at FleetMon for the Thames Estuary shipping data; Paul Mach for all the Strava data; and Laurence Holloway at Lovestruck for providing our data on dating. Thank you to Guy Simpson for the London Coffee Guide and Helen Wilson at the Booksellers Association for the list of independent bookshops in London. Special thanks to Junko Tateishi and Kazuko Minagawa at Bandai Namco for granting us permission to bring Pac-Man to London.

FROM JAMES: I would like to thank the Economic and Social Research Council for their funding of the Big Open Data: Mining and Synthesis (BODMAS) project. Without it I would not have had the resources to undertake the open data research behind many of the book's graphics, nor would I have had the opportunity to make a hugely enjoyable academic visit to Sara Fabrikant and colleagues at the University of Zurich in order to learn more about cartographic representations of data.

Thanks in large part to the energy of Mike Batty, CASA has become home to some of the best brains in London and has provided the perfect base for producing a book such as this. I would also like to thank Andrew Hudson-Smith for supporting my BODMAS application as well as Martin Zaltz-Austwick and Adam Dennett for arranging cover for my teaching. From the UCL Department of Geography,

I'm particularly grateful to Paul Longley for his on-going academic mentorship.

Special thanks go to Rob, William, Lydia, Kat, Chris, Kat, Holly, Jill, Allen and Mali who heard me talk about little else for a year. Thanks to Letty for being a great friend and for sorting the prescription drugs.

No words (or graphics!) can express my heartfelt gratitude to Isla for being with me every step of the way. I could not have embarked on this project without her. Lastly, I would like to thank my parents for their support and encouragement; without it, I would not have the confidence to pursue my ambitions.

FROM OLIVER: This book may be about London, but for me it bears testament to the comforts of another city: Ann Arbor, Michigan in the US. Every page of this book was designed there, either in my studio or at my favourite haunts, namely Literati Bookstore, 826Michigan, Zingerman's and The Espresso Bar. Without design assistance from Corinn Lewis and the love and support of my mother, brother, Sophie, Barrington, Jenny, Amy, Casey, Vince, Phil and Erin, my psyche surely would have crumbled. I would be remiss not to thank my friends and mentors at *National Geographic* – David, Susan, Maggie, Juan, Fernando, John, Sean and Bill – whose influence appears on all of these pages.

Finally, we both must thank our agent Luigi Bonomi for his enthusiasm from day one and for putting us in touch with the team at Particular Books/Penguin who shared our passion for the project. We are grateful to Helen Conford and Cecilia Stein for their editorial guidance, Jim Stoddart for advice on the cover design and James Blackman for his expertise on printing, binding and colour production. We feel lucky to have been paired with a team that believes books can and should be beautiful objects.

'I can never understand why Londoners fail to see that they live in the most wonderful city in the world.'

—Bill Bryson, *Notes from a Small Island*

Bill Bryson published these words in 1995,
when London was only at the beginning of its most recent
ascendancy. It was a time before London had its own mayor,
before it built landmarks like the London Eye and Tate Modern,
before the energy of the 2012 Olympics.

In the years since, there have been dark times,
not least the terrorist attacks of July 2005 and ongoing issues
of social equality that reignited in the summer riots of 2011.
Despite these setbacks, there is a real sense that London is
recognising its strengths, and for the second time in its history,
has over 8 million reasons to feel optimistic.

Hello!

Welcome to London, or as its residents might say:

¡Bienvenido a Londres!
Landana sbāgatama!
Witamy w Londynie!
Mirë se vini në Londër!
Välkommen till London!
Laṇṭan̲ varavēr̲kir̲ōm!
Kalós ílthate sto Londíno!
Londra'ya hoşgeldiniz!
Rondon e yōkoso!
Kaabo si London!

To view the capital's linguistic diversity in greater detail, see pp. 104–105.

SOURCE: 2011 CENSUS, ONS

kem cho · kem cho · kem cho · kem cho · salut · kem cho · kem cho · kem cho · kem cho · kem cho · kem cho · kem cho · kem cho · cześć · kem cho · kem cho · kem cho · kem cho · kem cho · kem cho · vanakkam · kem cho · kem cho · kem cho · kem cho · kem cho · kem cho · kem cho · kem cho · vanakkam · vanakkam · kem cho · kem cho · kem cho · cześć · vanakkam · vanakkam · kem cho · kem cho · kem cho · vanakkam · cześć · kem cho · haye · ni hao · cześć · cześć · cześć · cześć · kem cho · cześć · cześć · cześć · kem cho · haye · ni hao · sat sri akal · cześć · kem cho · sat sri akal · sat sri akal · cześć · cześć · cześć · haye · sat sri akal · sat sri akal · sat sri akal · cześć · cześć · ola · cześć · sat sri akal · sat sri akal · cześć · cześć · cześć · cześć · sat sri akal · sat sri akal · cześć · cześć · konnichiwa · cześć · sat sri akal · sat sri akal · sat sri akal · cześć · cześć · cześć · cześć · sat sri akal · sat sri akal · sat sri akal · cześć · cześć · cześć · cześć · sat sri akal · sat sri akal · sat sri akal · cześć · cześć · cześć · cześć · sat sri akal · sat sri akal · cześć · cześć · sat sri akal · sat sri akal · cześć · hola · cz · sat sri akal · sat sri akal · cześć · hola · sat sri akal · sat sri akal · cześć · cześć · guten tag · sat sri akal · cześć · cześć · guten tag haye dorood kem cho merhaba merhaba merhaba merhaba assalam-o-alekum cześć merhaba

salut kem cho czesc czesc merhaba merhaba merhaba merhaba assalam-o-alekum czesc assalam-o-alekum merhaba merhaba merhaba

cześć dorood czesc czesc merhaba merhaba czesc czesc czesc assalam-o-alekum assalam-o-alekum

cześć shalom bonjour merhaba czesc merhaba merhaba czesc assalam-o-alekum

kem cho czesc ciao hola hola czesc sholem aleykhem assalam-o-alekum

kem cho czesc czesc bonjour merhaba merhaba sholem aleykhem czesc

czesc marhaban bonjour merhaba hola merhaba sholem aleykhem assalam-o-alekum czesc czesc czesc

czesc czesc dorood bonjour salaam hola merhaba merhaba kem cho assalam-o-alekum salaam

czesc czesc bonjour bonjour bonjour hola salaam merhaba merhaba merhaba czesc czesc salaam

olá marhaban bonjour bonjour salaam geia sou merhaba merhaba merhaba merhaba salaam salaam

marhaban marhaban bonjour salaam salaam merhaba merhaba merhaba merhaba salaam kem cho

marhaban marhaban konnichiwa bonjour salaam merhaba merhaba merhaba salaam salaam kem cho

olá olá marhaban marhaban bonjour salaam bonjour merhaba salaam salaam salaam salaam kem cho

marhaban marhaban salaam salaam bonjour merhaba salaam salaam salaam salaam salaam

marhaban marhaban marhaban marhaban salaam salaam bonjour merhaba salaam salaam salaam salaam salaam

haye marhaban marhaban marhaban bonjour hola salaam salaam salaam salaam

marhaban hola bonjour marhaban ni hao bonjour salaam salaam salaam salaam labas

River Thames

marhaban marhaban bonjour marhaban bonjour hola bonjour salaam salaam salaam labas

czesc czesc bonjour bonjour bonjour ni hao hola ni hao salaam salaam

bonjour bonjour bonjour ciao ni hao salaam hola hola ni hao salaam namaste

bonjour marhaban bonjour bonjour marhaban olá hola hola bonjour salaam salaam

bonjour marhaban bonjour bonjour bonjour marhaban hola hola hola bonjour salaam namaste

hej marhaban bonjour bonjour ciao hola olá hola hola hola ni hao bonjour namaste

bonjour bonjour marhaban hola olá olá olá hola ni hao olá bonjour

czesc bonjour bonjour bonjour ciao bonjour olá olá hola czesc bonjour bonjour merhaba

czesc hola haye bonjour olá olá olá hola bonjour czesc czesc bonjour

czesc hola assalam-o-alekum bonjour olá olá hola bonjour hola vanakkam czesc bonjour

INTRODUCTION

This book could not have been made ten years ago. Computers weren't powerful enough. Data weren't as detailed or freely available. Technologies like Twitter and smartphones did not exist. And, well, Oliver and I did not know each other.

His world of design and my world of mapping first united in 2010 when he was working at *National Geographic*. I was studying for a Ph.D. that focused on the geographic patterns of millions of surnames in Europe and beyond. Oliver contacted me for help producing a map of the most popular surnames in the US. When the resulting graphic was short-listed for the 'Information is Beautiful' awards in 2012, Oliver flew to London for the event and stopped by my office at University College London's Centre for Advanced Spatial Analysis to say hello. On that day, the collaboration for this book was born: What if we took all the data we could find – on happiness, house prices, art, violent crime, life expectancy – and created a new visual guide to London for the twenty-first century?

All cities can be captured in maps that depict street layouts or the locations of landmarks, but London is a city *defined* by them. Its maps are special. They were drawn by pioneers such as Charles Booth, who revealed the full extent of the city's poverty, and Phyllis Pearsall, who mapped 23,000 streets in her hugely popular *A to Z* guide. But the map Londoners are probably most familiar with belongs to Henry Beck. His 1931 Tube map eschewed geographic accuracy for a more diagrammatic display of the city's Underground lines. Instantly recognizable the world over, it remains one of the most beloved representations of the capital. Its multicoloured lines have become part of the urban fabric alongside London's red buses and black cabs. Remove maps from London and you damage the city itself.

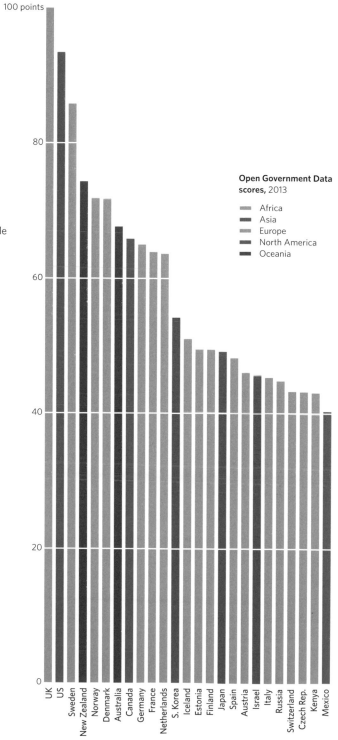

100 points

The UK tops this list of the world's most 'open' countries. To determine these rankings, the World Wide Web Foundation and Open Data Institute analyzed the data-sharing capacity of each country's government, businesses and citizens; the extent of published datasets; and their political, economic and social impact

Open Government Data scores, 2013

- Africa
- Asia
- Europe
- North America
- Oceania

The Information Capital

Referring to London as *the* information capital is a bold claim. We think it is justified for two reasons: London not only generates a huge volume of data, it *shares* an unprecedented amount with its citizens to use as they wish. These data are known as 'open data' and in recent years, the UK government has made their dissemination a national priority. Open data initiatives exist in other cities, not least in Europe and North America, but what gives London an information edge is the belief that data can not only record social change but also instigate it.

Back in 2009, a now legendary (in the data world at least) exchange over

SOURCE: WEB FOUNDATION, OPEN DATA BAROMETER 2013 GLOBAL REPORT dinner is said to have taken place between Gordon Brown, then Prime Minister, and Sir Tim Berners-Lee, inventor of the World Wide Web. Brown asked Berners-Lee how the government should make best use of the Web. Berners-Lee said that it should put all of its data online. Much to his surprise, the Prime Minister replied, 'Yeah, let's do it.' Since then, London and, in turn, many UK cities have created online data stores, sites where anyone can go to download data on everything from unemployment to cycle ridership. Berners-Lee went on to co-found the Open Data Institute, a London-based non-profit facilitating positive change through the dissemination of data around the globe.

Thanks to the subsequent development of an 'Open Government License', the public can now 'copy, publish, distribute, transmit and adapt' the work of many Great British institutions, not least the Office for National Statistics (ONS) and Ordnance Survey, Great Britain's national mapping agency. The ONS administers the census programme for England and Wales, releasing data at the finest geographic scales possible. Using data from the 2011 Census, for example, we were able to plot the ethnicities of Londoners within 25,000 small areas, each home to around 250 people (see pp. 100–101).

In 1995, Ordnance Survey finished digitizing 230,000 paper maps, making Great Britain the first country to store all its most detailed maps electronically. Their 1,200 employees continue to survey and record the changing landscape, a task that requires up to 4,000 data edits per day. Not all of Ordnance Survey's data are open, but those that are cover a huge range of uses and applications, including every building outline in this book.

The final reason for London's openness – alongside all the data from social media and transport networks – are the Freedom of Information Requests (FOIs) overseen by the Information Commissioner's Office (see right). FOIs came into

Freedom of Information requests on *whatdotheyknow.com*
January 2008 – June 2014

1 500 1,000 1,500 2,000

Successful

Unsuccessful or outstanding

Since its launch in 2008, *whatdotheyknow.com* has fielded more than 210,000 FOI requests for information from 15,000 authorities. Here we show the forty London authorities that receive the most requests.

Transport for London
Metropolitan Police Service
Westminster City Council
Camden Council
Lambeth Council
Newham Council
Tower Hamlets Council
Hackney Council
Islington Council
Croydon Council
Barnet Council
Haringey Council
Brent Council
Southwark Council
Greenwich Council
Wandsworth Council
Harrow Council
Hammersmith and Fulham Council
Hillingdon Council
Bexley Council
Royal Borough of Kensington and Chelsea
Lewisham Council
Barking and Dagenham Council
Ealing Council
Bromley Council
Waltham Forest Council
Enfield Council
Richmond upon Thames Council
Hounslow Council
Redbridge Council
Merton Council
Havering Council
Sutton Council
Kingston upon Thames Council
City of London Corporation
Greater London Authority
City of London Police
Common Council of the City of London
West London Mental Health NHS Trust
University College London

Jan-Mar Apr-Jun

2009   2010   2011   2012   2013   2014

2,025 requests
985 fulfilled

Jul–Sept   Oct–Dec   Jan–Mar   Apr–Jun   Jul–Sept   Oct–Dec   Jan–Mar   Apr–Jun   Jul–Sept   Oct–Dec   Jan–Mar   Apr–Jun   Jul–Sept   Oct–Dec   Jan–Mar   Apr–Jun   Jul–Sept   Oct–Dec   Jan–Mar   Apr–Jun   Jul–Sept   Oct–Dec   Jan–Mar   Apr–Jun force with the Freedom of Information Act 2000. Since then, they have been used by all sections of society, from members of the public wondering how their taxes are spent to journalists fishing for major scandals. Each request has to be made in writing, a process made much simpler by *whatdotheyknow.com*. Launched in 2008, the site now handles 20% of all requests to the UK central government. As we show on page 23, use is increasing.

Once a request has been made, the relevant agency is legally obligated to respond within twenty working days. If there's an unexplained delay – as there was with our request to Transport for London for data on, appropriately, Tube delays – then an internal review can be requested. If the review doesn't speed things along, the case goes before the 'Information Commissioner', who has powers to solicit a response. Not all requests can be fulfilled though. Organizations may deny requests that reveal sensitive information or prove unreasonably time-consuming for staff to complete. But without FOIs, we wouldn't have been able to produce our graphics on Tube delays, police helicopters and the London Fire Brigade, among others.

In addition to these 'official' sources of data, Londoners volunteer much more through the likes of fitness apps, social media and a user-generated mapping platform called OpenStreetMap (OSM), which is like Wikipedia for roads and buildings. Its founder and fellow Londoner, Steve Coast, placed the first OSM data point in Regent's Park in 2004 (see p. 27). Since then, OSM's thousands of active users have created a comprehensive map of London and much of the planet. The result is a living map that constantly evolves in sync with the world it seeks to represent as users add new information about anything that interests them, from new road junctions through to their favourite coffee shop, even the trees in their neighbourhood (see pp. 48–49).

OpenStreetMap echoes many of London's great mapping endeavours: it began

AREA ENLARGED

Today, London uses an Index of Multiple Deprivation to identify poorer areas in the capital. A century earlier, Charles Booth's 'poverty map' coloured streets 'according to the general condition of the inhabitants'. More colours meant the street contained 'a fair proportion of each of the classes represented by the respective colours'.

Index of Multiple Deprivation by decile, 2010

MOST DEPRIVED

LEAST DEPRIVED

Booth's poverty map, 1889

LEAST DEPRIVED

Upper-middle and Upper classes. Wealthy.

Middle-class. Well-to-do.

Fairly comfortable. Good ordinary earnings.

Mixed. Some comfortable, others poor.

Poor. 18s. to 21s. a week for a moderate family.

Very poor, casual. Chronic want.

Lowest class. Vicious, semi-criminal.

MOST DEPRIVED

SOURCES: DEPARTMENT FOR COMMUNITIES AND LOCAL GOVERNMENT (INDICES OF DEPRIVATION); LIBRARY OF THE LONDON SCHOOL OF ECONOMICS AND POLITICAL SCIENCE (BOOTH)

The founder of OpenStreetMap placed its first point in Regent's Park. --

with boots on the ground. Charles Booth looked to those who walked London most – policemen and school board inspectors – to provide the data on his maps of poverty (see p. 25); and Phyllis Pearsall is said to have walked all 23,000 streets in her *A-Z*. With the exception of Oliver's hikes to all thirteen of London's Protected Vistas (see pp. 68-73), we spent more time pounding the keyboard than the pavements. For this book, we were largely recipients rather than producers of data. This created a paradox. While more of London's data are available than ever before, the bar was set a little higher for us to make full use of them. To sift through spreadsheets millions of rows long, computer programming and data mining are now essential skills for cartographers. That said, the need to tell a story

alongside the graphics remains of utmost importance. For us, it was not enough to write scripts to generate patterns from data points. We tried to go the next step to help you understand what the patterns mean. If open data are to have the societal impact Berners-Lee envisions, this step is crucial.

Mapping the paths of London's shipping lanes (pp. 120–123) or jogging routes (pp. 154–7) required some of most technologically advanced plots ever produced for the capital, but technology is no substitute for pen and paper. Before we wrote a line of computer code or bent a single Bezier curve, we sketched up and talked through our approaches with the mantra 'just because we can, doesn't mean we

With thousands of
people contributing
millions of data points,
OpenStreetMap keeps
pace with the city's
constant changes.
Here we assigned
unique colours to
25 major contributors
in recognition of their
commitment to
mapping London.

0   5 km

SOURCES: OLIVER O'BRIEN, UNIVERSITY COLLEGE LONDON; OSM

Adam Towle, an architect on the Greater London Authority Regeneration team (with red laces) shows us Queen Elizabeth Olympic Park on a 160m² map in City Hall.

should'. To this end, you will find several 'low-tech' graphics in here, too. Perhaps the lowest-tech element of this book, however, is the book itself. Why print a book of maps when you can make them interactive online? Digital maps gain interactivity at the expense of tangibility and, we think, engagement. We wanted to create an object you could sit with, pore over, share with your friends (in person) and then discuss. Plus, print is still a pretty incredible technology. You can simply see more at a glance on a printed page than you can pinching, tapping and scrolling on a smartphone screen.

To see the power of print up close, head over to City Hall, the headquarters of the Greater London Authority. One of the largest printed maps of London has been pasted to its ground floor. Commissioned in time for the 2012 Olympics and produced from aerial photos taken by Ordnance Survey, it shows the expanse of the capital in amazing detail (above). Instead of panning and zooming, you can walk over to your house or stand on your favourite landmark. It is also a statement of power; if visitors to City Hall were to question the extent of the Mayor's influence, then they can be sent to the ground floor and shown it!

Our efforts continue a conversation that reached a crescendo during the 1850s, when London was already on its way to becoming the information capital. If you had walked its streets then, you may have passed Florence Nightingale using her coxcomb plots to lobby for better sanitary conditions in military hospitals or

In these diagrams, epidemiologist and statistician William Farr plotted cycles of temperature and deaths from cholera from 1840-50. He noted that the circular form and colours make 'the diagram represent the facts in a striking manner to the eye'. At the time, Farr believed cholera was spread by miasma, or 'bad air', from the Thames. Although this hypothesis was incorrect, Farr left an important legacy. He set up the first national system for collecting statistics; he advocated a data-driven approach to public health; and he pioneered the graphic representation of such information.

AREA ENLARGED

PLAN

SHEWING THE ASCERTAINED DEATHS FROM CHOLERA

in part of the Parishes of

Sᵀ JAMES, WESTMINSTER,

AND

Sᵀ ANNE, SOHO,

DURING THE SUMMER AND AUTUMN OF 1854.

bumped into epidemiologist William Farr collecting data on the city's latest cholera mortalities. Farr was a great pioneer in the use and communication of statistics. He created polar area charts to support the theory that cholera was spread through 'bad air' blown in from the Thames (see p. 29). In spite of his data-driven approach to public health and creation of a national system for collecting statistics, his contribution is often obscured by another data visualization: John Snow's 'Ghost Map' (see right), which proved that the source of cholera was not the air as Farr posited, but London's water supply. Though much less colourful than Farr's graphic, it was – and remains – ruthlessly efficient at communicating the information. Snow grasped what Farr had missed: geography matters.

John Snow's *'Plan Showing the Ascertained Deaths from Cholera in Part of the Parishes of St. James, Westminster and St. Anne, Soho, during the summer and autumn of 1854'*, with the infamous Broad Street water pump at its centre, was the showpiece of a report that argued that cholera is a waterborne disease. This map inspired a revolution not only for medicine but also for the future of information design.

Using This Book

'Most A-Zs are half dead, because documenting a city as alive as London will always be an impossible task.'

—Craig Taylor, author of *Londoners*

This book is not an atlas. We have not sought to present a single, definitive picture of the city. Instead, we have selected 100 or so facets based on two simple questions: do we find it interesting and do we think you will too? In a city as diverse as London, there are many more graphics we would have loved to produce, but we had to draw the line somewhere or the book would have never been published.

As you read, please remember that each graphic marks a point in time. We have used the most current data available as of Spring 2014. Therefore, we encourage you to view the graphics as snapshots rather than graven definitions. Ultimately, we hope they will inspire conversations – and new graphics – about the city's future.

We collated our graphics around five themes: *where we are, who we are, where we go, how we're doing* and *what we like.* The structure is non-linear and the graphics stand alone, so jump around the book as you might on a day out in the city.

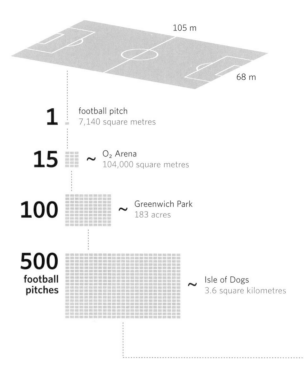

105 m

68 m

1 football pitch
7,140 square metres

15 ~ O₂ Arena
104,000 square metres

100 ~ Greenwich Park
183 acres

500 football pitches ~ Isle of Dogs
3.6 square kilometres

London is surprisingly vast. What appears to be a short stroll between Waterloo and Tower Bridges will take the better part of an hour to walk. In terms of area, the Isle of Dogs, the peninsula enclosed by the Thames' iconic meander, could hold 500 football pitches on it. The entire boundary of Greater London? 220,000 pitches.

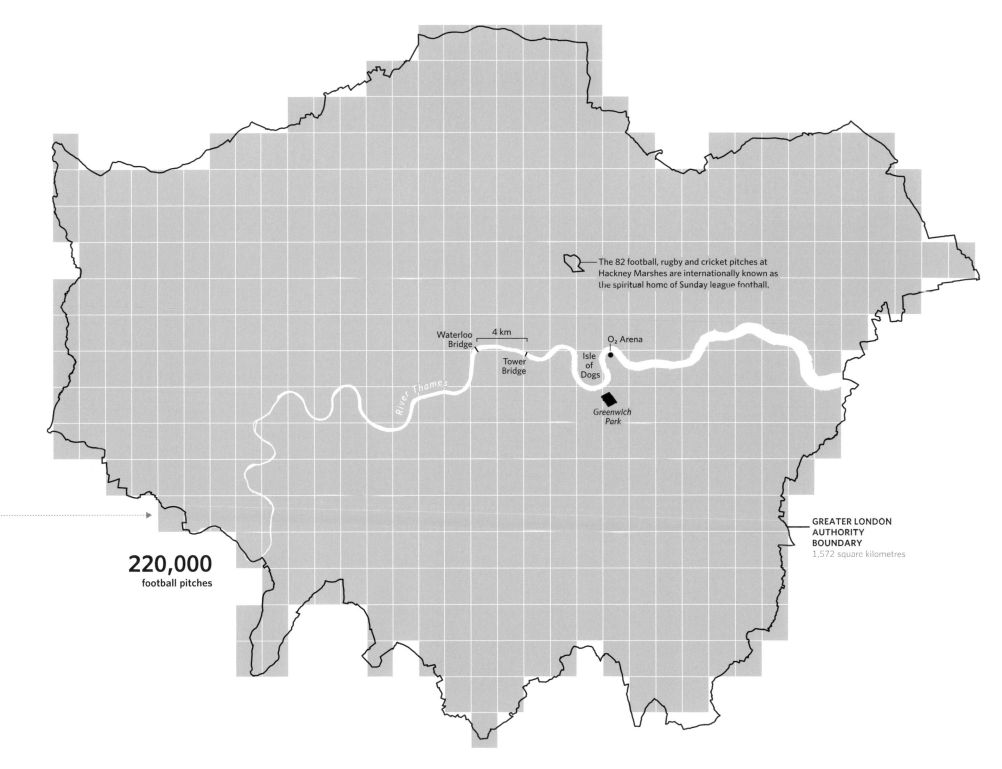

The 82 football, rugby and cricket pitches at Hackney Marshes are internationally known as the spiritual home of Sunday league football.

Waterloo Bridge

4 km

O₂ Arena

Tower Bridge

Isle of Dogs

River Thames

Greenwich Park

220,000
football pitches

GREATER LONDON AUTHORITY BOUNDARY
1,572 square kilometres

1 WHERE WE ARE

THE CHILTERNS

To St Albans

To Lincoln and York

To Stevenage

LEA VALLEY

ERMINE STREET

River Roding

Bushey Heath
153m

Brockley
Hill
136m

+ Stanmore Hill
152m

Pole
Hill
91m

River Lea

WATLING STREET

Highgate Hill
136m

Hackney Brook

Dollis Hill
78m

+ Parliament Hill
98m

Fleet

Horsenden Hill
85m

Westbourne

+ Primrose Hill
64m

Tyburn

Walbrook Stream

Old Ford

Castlebar Hill
51m

+ Hanger Hill
65m

LONDON
WALL

Stamford Brook

River Thames

Counter's Creek

WATLING STREET

Telegraph Hill
48m

Shooters Hill
133m

Falcon Brook

Herne Hill
43m

Hilly Fields
51m

Richmond Hill
45m at Richmond Gate

Effra River

One Tree Hill
91m

River Crane

King
Henry's
Mound
56m

+ Spankers
Hill
42m

Coombe
Hill
54m

Ravensbourne

To Silchester

Beaulieu
Heights
116m

River Wandle

Addington
Hills
146m

River Darent

Winey
Hill
72m

Breakneck Hill
144m

PILGRIMS' WAY

Londinium, 300 A.D.

+ Elevated point

— Roman road

THE NORTH

0   5 km

Westerham Heights
245m

3 6

To Chichester

Box Hill
224m

To Brighton

To Lewes

Amersham
150m
Highest point
on London
Underground
network

M25

M25

M25

M25

M25

M25

Crews Hill

Mill Hill

Harold
Hill

Stamford Hill

Harrow-on-the-Hill

BT Tower
191m

Heron Tower
230m

One Canada
Square
235m

Beckton
Alps
17m

Notting
Hill

OXFORD STREET

Campden
Hill

The Shard
310m

Westminster
–32m
Lowest point
on London
Underground
network

Victoria
Tower
99m

QUEEN
ELIZABETH II
BRIDGE

The Thames shown
here is narrower and
deeper than it was
when the Romans
settled in the area.

GREATER LONDON
AUTHORITY
BOUNDARY

Crystal
Palace
Transmitter
219m tall

Croydon

London, 2014

● Town
■ Building
— Motorway

Caterham-on-the-Hill

Highest point
in London

Sevenoaks

To Colchester
The Roman capital before Londinium

River Crouch

Foulness Island

Plumtree Hill
57m

Southend-on-Sea

Canvey Island

Thames Estuary

North Sea

River Medway

Isle of Sheppey

Rochester

The Swale

To Margate

D O W N S

Canterbury

To Dover

Contours of the City

The shape of London follows the shape of the land.

The Romans were trailblazers. In the first century, they surveyed the Thames Basin and made a series of planning decisions that continue to affect our lives two thousand years later. The Thames needed to be bridged, so they chose a shallow point around the area now known as Westminster. Slightly downstream, with plentiful freshwater from the (now hidden) Walbrook stream and sufficient depth in the Thames for shipping, the port of Londinium was born. It became the hub of a series of spoke-like roads that passed through the Chilterns and North Downs to all corners of Britannia. Silchester Road lives on as Oxford Street whilst the City of London remains the domain of rich merchants. It is remarkable how a city can change so much and yet so little.

SOURCES: OS; OLIVER O'BRIEN; UNIVERSITY COLLEGE LONDON

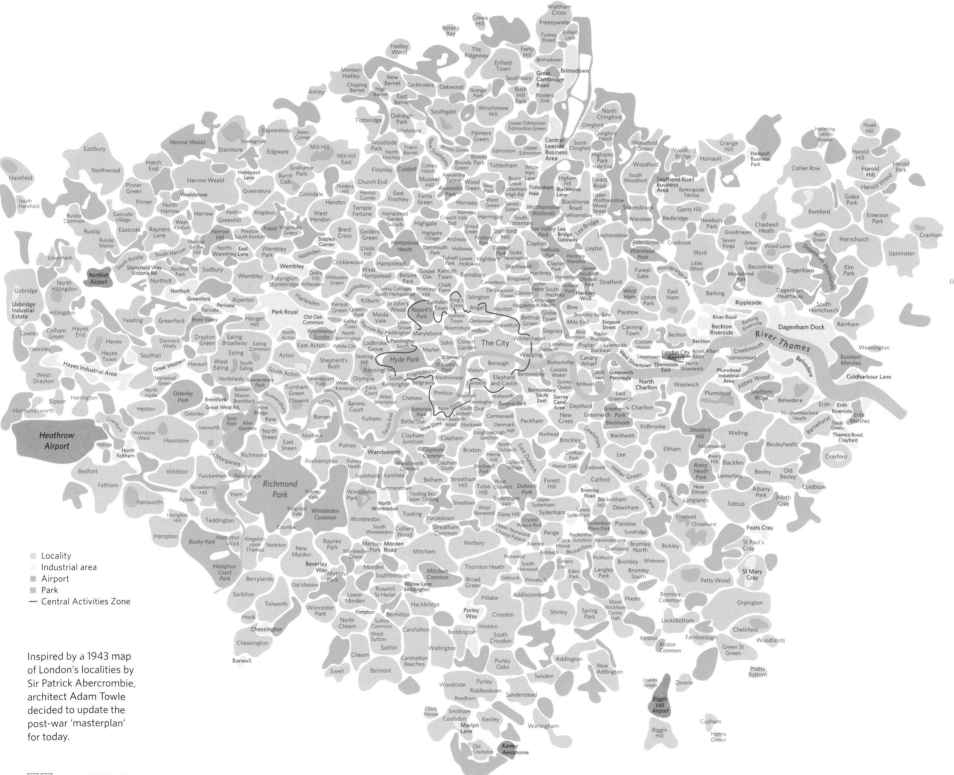

Locality
Industrial area
Airport
Park
— Central Activities Zone

Inspired by a 1943 map
of London's localities by
Sir Patrick Abercrombie,
architect Adam Towle
decided to update the
post-war 'masterplan'
for today.

What we talk about when we talk about London

Ask any two Londoners to define their city for you and you will probably get three different answers. So let's be clear. In this book, we're talking about a region known as the Greater London Authority (GLA). Created by the London Government Act 1963, it spans thirty-two boroughs plus the City of London, a 2,000-year-old city-within-a-city.

The GLA boundary forms the distinctive shape you see on the cover and throughout this book. To many people, however, its rounded arms and deckled edges – and the boroughs within them – are entirely arbitrary. They are social, economic and political creations designed to help govern the city. As individuals, we experience London with much more personal geographies.

In the map to the left, Adam Towle, an architect at City Hall, shows that we can further divide the GLA into a 'City of Villages' – 770 amoeba-shaped places where we live, work and play. They bear testament to the palimpsestic nature of London with names originating from a range of sources, including historic villages (Ealing), an anchorage for Danish invaders (Greenwich) and a 17th-century public house (Angel). As London has filled the spaces between its villages, their boundaries have blurred. Does spending the day in Camden Town now entail staying south of its lock or is there a more fluid boundary between Camden and Chalk Farm or Kentish Town? London's villages combine to form a city greater than the sum of its parts, but what keeps them unique?

We fumble for an answer because the extent and complexity of London varies in the minds of those who experience it. While no set of graphics could truly capture this diversity, many of the villages' unique characteristics appear throughout this book. As Peter Ackroyd writes in his biography of the city, 'London goes beyond any boundary or convention . . . It is illimitable.' In this sense, we use the GLA boundary not to limit our definition but as a lens through which we can focus the millions, if not billions, of data points available. At times we will zoom in on specific parts of the capital or zoom out for a wider perspective. Often we will return to London's distinctive administrative outline if only because it's a helpful tool for making comparisons and getting oriented.

In this chapter, we provide a few ways to visualize how London has evolved from an outpost of the Roman Empire to a truly global city. Its most rapid growth has been within the past 200 years, and it is still experiencing unprecedented demand from those who want to call it home. In the face of change, London remains sensitive to its past, preserving centuries-old views of St Paul's Cathedral and the street layout in the city centre. Perhaps the greatest continuity, though, is offered by the river flowing west to east past London's landmarks and acting as an enduring reminder of the city's link to nature. If you ever feel lost, look for 'Father Thames'.

Hub for the World

The sun never sets on an LHR luggage tag.

In terms of international air traffic, London is the centre of the world. Each year, a million flights set a course for 51°N, 0°W. Four of the six busiest airports in the UK share these coordinates. Each one services at least five continents, exchanging Londoners and British culture to places as far flung as Lagos, Brunei and Mauritius. But with nearly 70 million passengers and more than 200 destinations, Heathrow rules.

Built in the 1930s as a private airport, the 'Great West Aerodrome' expanded to its current size over the next fifty years. It has long since hit capacity. By travelling further afield, Gatwick, Stansted, Luton and London City Airport are bearing some of the load. Still, to meet projected demand, they're going to need reinforcements. Heathrow hopes to build a third runway. Mayor of London Boris Johnson envisions a new, larger airport in the middle of the Thames Estuary (see p. 119). If they build it, this airborne empire will have a new king.

69.5
million passengers
per year

LHR

Heathrow is not only the busiest airport in the UK, it handles more international traffic than any other airport globally. To do so requires a staff of more than 76,000 working around the clock. To see how flights descend into Heathrow, turn to page 116.

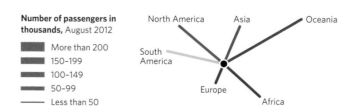

Number of passengers in thousands, August 2012

- More than 200
- 150–199
- 100–149
- 50–99
- Less than 50

North America · Asia · Oceania
South America
Europe · Africa

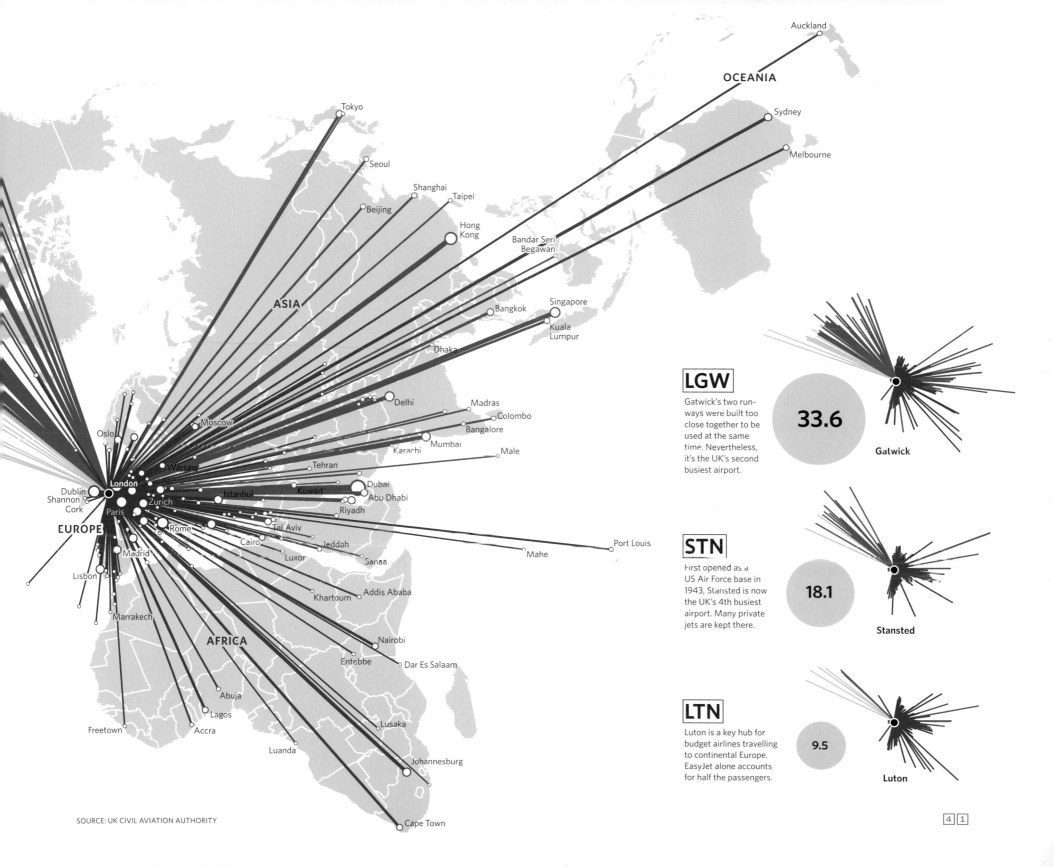

OCEANIA

Auckland

Sydney

Melbourne

ASIA

Tokyo
Seoul
Shanghai
Beijing
Taipei
Hong Kong
Bandar Seri Begawan
Bangkok
Singapore
Kuala Lumpur
Dhaka
Delhi
Madras
Colombo
Bangalore
Moscow
Mumbai
Karachi
Male
Tehran
Warsaw
Istanbul
Kuwait
Dubai
Abu Dhabi
Riyadh
Zurich
Tel Aviv
Cairo
Jeddah
Port Louis
Rome
Luxor
Mahe
Sanaa
Oslo
London
Dublin
Shannon
Cork
Paris
Madrid
Addis Ababa
Lisbon
Khartoum
Marrakech
Nairobi
Entebbe
Dar Es Salaam

EUROPE

AFRICA

Abuja
Lagos
Freetown
Accra
Luanda
Lusaka
Johannesburg
Cape Town

LGW

Gatwick's two run-ways were built too close together to be used at the same time. Nevertheless, it's the UK's second busiest airport.

33.6

Gatwick

STN

First opened as a US Air Force base in 1943, Stansted is now the UK's 4th busiest airport. Many private jets are kept there.

18.1

Stansted

LTN

Luton is a key hub for budget airlines travelling to continental Europe. EasyJet alone accounts for half the passengers.

9.5

Luton

SOURCE: UK CIVIL AVIATION AUTHORITY

From Home to Work

High-paying jobs draw workers from far, far away

In this depiction of daily commutes, London shines like the Sun in the constellation of Southern England. Like all stars, it has an immense gravitational pull. Whether by car, train or tube, thousands travel into the capital each day from all directions. Including this 'commuter belt' beyond the Greater London Authority boundary makes the capital one of the largest metropolitan areas in the EU with a population of more than 13 million.

Half of London's workforce make their journey by public transport, compared with only 9% in the rest of the country. Still, most need thirty minutes or more to get to work. Elsewhere in the UK, only 20% have commutes that long. Why do so many live so far away?

For one, London salaries go further in satellite towns like Banbury. As of May 2014, a five-bedroom converted barn there was going for the price of two-bedroom flats along the Underground's Central Line (see pp. 66–7). It's only a matter of time before faster trains propel commuters into even wider orbits.

Commuting times in minutes by region of workplace
October–December 2009

London   Rest of UK

WORCESTER

HEREFORD

CAMBRIDGE

Northampton

Ipswich

Milton
Keynes

Banbury

Felixstowe

Cheltenham

Luton

D

Colchester

GLOUCESTER

Aylesbury

Clacton-on-Sea

OXFORD

N

Harlow

ST ALBANS

CHELMSFORD

Swindon

*North
Sea*

Southend-on-Sea

BRISTOL

Reading

LONDON

Thames Estuary

A

Newbury

Rochester

Margate

BATH

Farnborough

Maidstone

Ramsgate

L

Basingstoke

Guildford

CANTERBURY

Ashford

SALISBURY

CRAWLEY

Tonbridge

Folkestone

G

WINCHESTER

N

Hastings

SOUTHAMPTON

BRIGHTON

Eastbourne

PORTSMOUTH

Bournemouth

Newport

English Channel

Weymouth

SCOTLAND

ENGLAND

WALES London

AREA ENLARGED

Day and Night

Commuters send the City's population off the charts.

London is a city of extremes. Just look at the difference in its daytime and nighttime populations. Using data from the 2011 Census, the top map shows the number of people by place of employment; the bottom one, by place of residence. In one corner of the City of London, the population spikes from 222 residents by night to in excess of 127,000 by day. How do they all fit? The only way is up in the rising number of skyscrapers (see pp. 68–73). By late evening, the pattern reverses. Workers head home and the City becomes eerily quiet.

CITY OF LONDON

Canary
Wharf

Covent
Garden

Oxford
Circus

BARNET

HARROW

ROMFORD

ILFORD

River Thames

River Thames

Heathrow Airport

ROMFORD

DAGENHAM

WALTHAMSTOW

ORPINGTON

LEA VALLEY

TOTTENHAM

BROMLEY

BIGGIN HILL

BRIXTON

PURLEY

CROYDON

KILBURN

FULHAM

EALING

KINGSTON

UXBRIDGE

FELTHAM

DAY

Not everyone works in the City. Smaller centres such as Harlow and Croydon host many workers, while Heathrow Airport employs thousands. Canary Wharf, the City's younger sibling, is on its way up.

NIGHT

Central London empties outwards to breathe life into the likes of Uxbridge and Romford. With few residents, the Lea Valley cuts a canyon between Tottenham and Walthamstow.

WHERE WE ARE

M25/M11 Junction
This junction shows the warmth of roads compared to surrounding countryside.

BARNET

ENFIELD

King George's Reservoir

ROMFORD

Alexandra Palace

HARROW

Hampstead Heath

Wembley Stadium

Victoria Park

Westfield Stratford City

UXBRIDGE

Regent's Park

Euston Station

St Paul's Cathedral

EALING

Paddington Station

London Eye

Tower of London

Canary Wharf

London City Airport

Hyde Park

SOUTHBANK

River Thames

Temperatures at Heathrow hit an all time high in August 2003 when they soared to 37.9°C (100.2°F).

Buckingham Palace

Waterloo Station

The Shard

Greenwich Park

Heathrow Airport

Battersea Park

Richmond Park

Parks are the coolest places to be on a midsummer night.

CRYSTAL PALACE

Bushy Park

BROMLEY

0   5 km

CROYDON

4 6

Hot Spots

If the climate continues to warm, Londoners will feel the heat.

London's abundance of concrete, glass and tarmac can turn an often cool city into a summer hot-house. It's what climatologists call the Urban Heat Island Effect. These dry, exposed surfaces accumulate energy from the sun during the day and then release it slowly overnight, which can lead to extreme temperature differences between the city and surrounding countryside. In this infrared image, all that released heat appears as bubbling lava, oozing eastwards through the River Thames. Purple blotches indicate cooler areas like parks and woodland. Elevated temperatures, particularly in the summer, can amplify energy usage (as people crank up their air conditioners) and instances of health problems like heatstroke. On the hottest days of the year it's actually good to get off the island.

Tilbury
Docks

Northfleet
Power
Station

With their cooling towers and limited green space, the Tilbury Docks and Northfleet Power Station glow bright on this map.

Surface temperatures
12 July 2006

—27°C
—25
—23
—21
—19
—17
—15
—13°C

Average temperatures rarely exceed 25°C in London, but on 12 July – a clear day at the start of 2006's hottest week – they rose to 27°.

19 July
Hottest day of the year: 35°

12 July
Date of image

30°

DAYTIME TEMPERATURES

20°

10°

NIGHTTIME TEMPERATURES

0°

JANUARY   FEBRUARY   MARCH   APRIL   MAY   JUNE   JULY   AUGUST   SEPTEMBER   OCTOBER   NOVEMBER   DECEMBER

SOURCES: THE LUCID PROJECT; WEATHERSPARK.COM (CHART DATA)

Barnet

Enfield

LONDON OUTER
ORBITAL PATH

LEA
VALLEY
WALK

*Epping
Forest*

Alexandra
Palace

Romford

Tottenham

CAPITAL
RING

*Walthamstow
Wetlands*

*Thames Chase
Community Forest*

*Colne Valley
Regional Park*

*Hampstead
Heath*

*Hackney
Marshes*

Emirates
Stadium

Queen Elizabeth
Olympic Park

Uxbridge

*Regent's
Park*

Victoria
Park

JUBILEE
WALKWAY

JUBILEE
GREENWAY

LEA
VALLEY
WALK

Hyde Park

Tower
of London

Canary
Wharf

London
Eye

*Osterley
Park*

Buckingham
Palace

*Battersea
Park*

*Greenwich
Park*

SOUTHEAST LONDON
GREEN CHAIN

*Kew
Gardens*

THAMES
PATH

**Heathrow
Airport**

Bexleyheath

*Clapham
Common*

*Dulwich
Park*

*Richmond
Park*

*Wimbledon
Common*

CAPITAL
RING

THAMES
PATH

Wimbledon

*Crystal
Palace Park*

*Bushy
Park*

*Mitcham
Common*

Croydon

*High Elms
County Park*

LONDON OUTER
ORBITAL PATH

Walking trails, 2014

 · · · · · · Paths

 ⌐⌐⌐⌐⌐ Loop trails

0   5 km

**GREATER LONDON
AUTHORITY
BOUNDARY**

Biggin Hill

The Urban Wild

Greater London is greener than you may think.

Londoners refer to the ring of woodland and open space encircling the Greater London Authority as a 'green belt', a restraining device set up in 1935 to keep the city's buildings from sprawling into the countryside. Within this green binding, however, London offers a patchwork of parks, reserves, World Heritage Sites and waterways that could be stitched together into something more: a national park.

Measuring 1,600 square-kilometres, Greater London National Park (as proposed by geographer Daniel Raven-Ellison) would be the seventh-largest in the UK and make London the world's first National Park city. 'There is this idea that a National Park has to be remote and rural,' says Raven-Ellison, 'but cities are incredibly important habitats too. An amazing 13,000 species of wildlife can be found in London's open spaces.' It's all possible because much of the infrastructure is already in place, including a 245-kilometre orbital footpath that, like a line of thread, weaves its way along the outer fringe.

In this false-colour satellite image taken on 14 March 2014, near-infrared, red and green wavelengths combine to make dense green vegetation appear red. Look closely and you'll see crimson specks within Olympic Stadium and Emirates Stadium, home of Arsenal Football Club (circled). Richmond Park still appears a bit brown because the trees were not yet in leaf.

SOURCE: NASA; MATHIAS DISNEY, UNIVERSITY COLLEGE LONDON; WALKING LONDON (PATHS). SHAREGEO OPEN (GREEN BELT)

Holding Back the Tide

It took a few floods to re-learn how to live with Father Thames.

If the Thames Barrier didn't exist, here's what could happen to the city. First, heavy rainfall swells the river. Then high tide or a storm surge pushes the excess water back upriver and over embankments. The threat isn't new. For most of London's history, these banks were uninhabited marshes that absorbed rising waters. But the Victorians seem to have buried that knowledge when they built up the Embankments in the early 19th century. On 7 January 1928, nature reasserted its power. The river burst its banks, drowning fourteen and leaving thousands homeless. Lesson learned? Not quite. It wasn't until a North Sea surge inundated Silvertown in 1953 that plans for a new defence system began.

CAMDEN TOWN

ISLINGTON

SOMERS TOWN

Regent's Park

BLOOMSBURY

CITY

St Paul's Cathedral

King's College

MAYFAIR

VICTORIA EMBANKMENT

Trafalgar Square

Tate Modern

SOUTHWARK

The Shard

Green Park

Waterloo Station

London Eye

St James's Park

Houses of Parliament

Buckingham Palace

Westminster Abbey

Lambeth Palace

Elephant and Castle

KENSINGTON

BROMPTON

WESTMINSTER

Tate Britain

ALBERT EMBANKMENT

KENNINGTON

WALWORTH

EARLS COURT

CHELSEA

WEST KENSINGTON

WEST BROMPTON

CHELSEA EMBANKMENT

River Thames

Stamford Bridge Chelsea F. C.

Battersea Park

New Covent Garden Market

WALHAM GREEN

PARSONS GREEN

Victoria Park

BOW

BETHNAL
GREEN

STEPNEY

POPLAR

ExCeL London

ROTHERHITHE
TUNNEL

Tower
of London

BLACKWALL
TUNNEL

London City
Airport

City Hall

Canary Wharf

O₂
Arena

SILVERTOWN

BERMONDSEY

ROTHERHITHE

Thames
Barrier

Southwark
Park

ISLE OF DOGS

Burgess
Park

DEPTFORD

River Thames

GREENWICH

Greenwich
Park

HOW THE THAMES BARRIER WORKS
On days with high flooding risk, ten steel
gates, each 15 metres tall, rotate up from
the riverbed at low tide to prevent water
from flowing upriver. They remain in this
closed position until the tide recedes.

Of all the barrier closures since its
completion in 1982, one-fifth occurred in
early 2014 when 250 millimetres of rain
fell in two months.

0   1 km

Areas with a 1% risk of
flooding per year

SOURCES: ENVIRONMENT AGENCY; OS (BUILDINGS)

If These Streets Could Talk

You can't turn a corner in London without stepping through time.

In 1685, London's street plan didn't look too different from the one laid down by the Romans. Then when the population rose to six million in the following centuries, new streets were built as the city spread and became a stomping ground for many famous names.

Many Londoners have heard of John Snow, the physician-turned-epidemiologist who ended a cholera outbreak in 1854 by tracing its source to a water pump on what is now Soho's Broadwick Street. They might also know of William Caslon, who designed the serif fonts on this map at his type foundry on Chiswell Street. But what about Lord Rowton, Robert Adam or The Old Nichol slum? Ken 'Old Map Man' Titmuss can tell you all about them and he'll show you around town for a tenner. 'My walks celebrate everyday London and the many unsung local heroes,' he says. Here he shares six of his lesser-known stories from the streets.

Historic Streets
— 1685
— 1880

PADDINGTON

BAYSWATER

NOTTING HILL

Kensington Gardens

Holland Park

KENSINGTON

HAMMERSMITH

EARLS COURT

WEST KENSINGTON

WEST BROMPTON

CASTELNAU

WALHAM GREEN

BARNES

PARSONS GREEN

PUTNEY

WANDSWORTH

1 STRATFORD PLACE

This cul-de-sac takes you back to 1236 A.D. when the City of London constructed a conduit here to divert water from the River Tyburn to the City. Around 1553, a hunting lodge was built to house the Lord Mayor and his Aldermen when they rode out to inspect the conduits. Once the New River aqueduct opened in 1613, the Tyburn conduit fell out of use and the lodge was demolished. Edward Stratford leased the site in 1771 and built a grand house that is now home to the Oriental Club.

2 CHANDOS STREET

Follow this street until it curves and you will find a house with two Doric columns. Completed in 1771, it's the first London house designed by the Scottish neoclassical architect Robert Adam and his brother John. The house owes its unusual shade of grey to the Adam brothers' choice of stone from the Craigleith Quarry near Edinburgh, where they grew up. When it was first put up for sale there were no buyers. Now its current tenant, the Royal Society of Medicine, hires out the house for weddings.

3 CRAVEN STREET

Walk along this street where Benjamin Franklin once lived, and you will find a blue plaque for another famous American: Herman Melville. Having published his first book Typee in London, Melville returned in 1849 to place his fifth novel, White-Jacket. At 25 Craven Street, Mrs Morgan's lodging house gave him a base from which to visit agents and explore the city. There was no Embankment yet, so the seafaring author could walk down to the river via steps at the end of the street.

4 BONDWAY

Walking south from Vauxhall Bus Station, you will find a large brick structure about halfway along with narrow windows and the date 1892 above the door. This is the first of six hostels built specifically for working men by philanthropist Lord Rowton. Having undertaken a survey of lodging houses while private secretary to Prime Minister Disraeli, Rowton saw room for improvement. His Rowton Houses provided clean sheets, washing facilities, hot water and a meal for sixpence a night.

5 BERMONDSEY STREET

Enter the churchyard of St Mary Magdalen and look for the building in the corner where Bermondsey meets Abbey. This dates to 1812 and was built as the Watch House. Once common, these are now rare buildings. The Watch House had two functions. First, it enabled parish constables to keep an eye on the churchyard. Secondly, it provided the church with a lock-up to detain those found sleeping rough in the yard. In some parts of London, the Watch House went on to be the Town Hall.

6 ARNOLD CIRCUS

In the 1890s, the London County Council designed its first housing project, the Boundary Estate, on the site of The Old Nichol slum – and they made Arnold Circus the centrepiece: four-storey mansion blocks radiating off a central garden, its mound formed from the rubble of the slums. Though the estate housed more than 5,000, only eleven residents of Old Nichol could afford to live there.

SOURCE: KEN TITMUSS; KIRIL STANILOV, UNIVERSITY OF CAMBRIDGE (STREET DATA)

Cross-section along Crossrail route

PADDINGTON STATION

BT TOWER

CENTRE POINT

CITY OF LONDON

Royal Oak
*Bison bones
68,000 years ago*

*To Reading
and Heathrow*

Royal Oak

Tottenham Court Road
*8,000 jars
19th–20th century*

Charterhouse Square
*Black Death victims
14th century*

Liverpool Street
*Roman skull, horse skull
300–400 AD*

Davies Street
*Bone or ivory domino
18th or 19th century*

Farringdon
*Shoe
Mid-16th century*

Paddington

Farringdon

Whitechapel

Bond Street

Liverpool Street

Davies St

Charterhouse
Square

Tottenham Court Road

Dean Street
*Tobacco pipe
1580s*

Liverpool Street
*Bone, glass and amber
beaded necklace
16th–18th century*

Planned Crossrail route, 2014

━━━ Tunnel
╥╥╥╥ Surface line
◎◎ Stations

Liverpool Street
*Ice skate
8th-16th century*

What Lies Beneath

Excavating Crossrail has brought London's buried history to the surface.

After thirty-five years of planning, the largest archaeology project in UK history broke ground on 15 May 2009. The 100-kilometre east-west railway, which requires tunnels between nine new stations in Central London, grants researchers an opportunity to travel down London's complex and varied timeline. 'Construction and archaeology may not have gone hand-in-hand in the past,' says Crossrail's chief archaeologist Jay Carver, 'but together, this collaboration has produced 10,000 previously undiscovered artefacts.' Here we show some of his top finds. The oldest? Pieces of fossilized resin that oozed from a tree 55 million years ago.

FOOD PACKAGING
An underground vault beneath a former Crosse & Blackwell food company warehouse near Tottenham Court Road revealed around 8,000 unused ceramic and stoneware jars for pickles, marmalade and sauces.

BURIAL GROUNDS
Carver's team has found hundreds of skeletons beneath the City, including plague victims and skulls that eroded from a Roman cemetery on the banks of the former Walbrook stream (see pp. 36-7). They expect to find more.

SOURCE: CROSSRAIL. SKETCHES: OLIVER UBERTI

CANARY WHARF

O₂ ARENA

WEST INDIA DOCK

RIVER LEA

RIVER THAMES

To Shenfield

Stratford

Pudding Mill Lane

Liverpool Street
Roman coins
119–316 AD

Stepney Green
junction

River Lea

Canary Wharf
Mammoth jawbone
20,000 years ago

WEST INDIA DOCK

Canary Wharf

Amber
55 million years ago

Limmo
Peninsula

Stepney Green
Chamber pot
19th century

Stepney Green
Tudor bowling balls
16th century

River Roding

North Woolwich
Mesolithic flint scraper
7,000–4,000 BC

Custom House

VICTORIA DOCK

North
Woolwich

River Thames

CROSS SECTION
ABOVE

Woolwich

To Abbey Wood

Plumstead

PREHISTORIC CREATURES
Mammoths, reindeer and bison
once grazed along London's waterways. Gnaw marks on their bones
suggest the animals were washed
away in floodwaters and then
scavenged by carnivores before
being preserved in sediment.

FLINT & STEEL
Crossrail's tunnel-boring machines
have unearthed far older technologies: Stone Age flint scrapers;
cannons at the Royal Arsenal in
North Woolwich; and foundations
from the 19th-century Thames
Ironworks on Limmo Peninsula.

Ghosts of London Past

Two thousand years of history haunts the city's streets and structures.

Phasmophobic? Then you may want to make like Pac-Man and avoid the ghosts on this map. Otherwise follow the dots to tour centuries of paranormal activity, including victims of Jack the Ripper, the Tower executioner and the Blitz. For extra points, grab some cherries at Borough Market or a cocktail at Apples & Pears.

1 Phantom Bus
A spectral No. 7 troubles the corner of Cambridge Gardens and St Marks Road.

2 Crocker's Folly
Former landlord Frank Crocker still stalks the abandoned pub, having supposedly taken his own life at the inn's failure.

3 The Volunteer
This pub is haunted by the Duke of Norfolk, whose mansion once stood on this site.

4 Langham Hotel
At least seven different ghosts have been attributed to room 333.

5 British Museum
The museum's tube station closed in 1933. It's now cursed by the wailing of Egyptian voices.

6 The Dolphin
Hit by a Zeppelin bomb in WWI, this pub's stopped clock can sometimes be heard ticking.

7 Farringdon
One of London's oldest stations harbours a screaming ghost, said to be murdered orphan Anne Naylor.

8 Sadler's Wells
The ghost of clown Grimaldi haunts a theatre box.

9 The Sutton Arms
A mischievous red-headed ghost has been sighted at this pub near the setting of the Sherlock Holmes tale, *The Red Headed League*.

10 Bethnal Green
Cries of those who perished in a wartime crush are still heard by Underground staff.

11 Bow Bells
The ladies' toilet at this pub flushes of its own accord.

12 50 Berkeley Square
London's most famous haunted house is said to have literally scared people to death.

13 Covent Garden
Actor William Terriss haunts the station, having been murdered nearby.

14 Peacock Theatre
Inside, you can hear the clicks and squeaks of a phantom dolphin, star of a Paul Raymond show in the 1960s.

15 Amen Court
A ghastly canine haunts this street, a shade of a former prisoner in Newgate Gaol.

16 Mitre Square
The ghost of Jack the Ripper victim Catherine Eddowes appears here, bearing her wounds.

17 Aldgate
The ghostly figure of a woman nursed a worker who'd received an electric shock. He later recovered.

18 Tower of London
More than a dozen phantoms dwell here, including Anne Boleyn, the Two Princes and a bear.

19 The Grenadier
Said to be among London's most haunted pubs, paranormal activity peaks in September.

20 Green Park
A black figure and pained voices have been witnessed near the park's 'Death Tree'.

21 The George
This 17th-century inn is haunted by a tech-hating landlady who might break your phone.

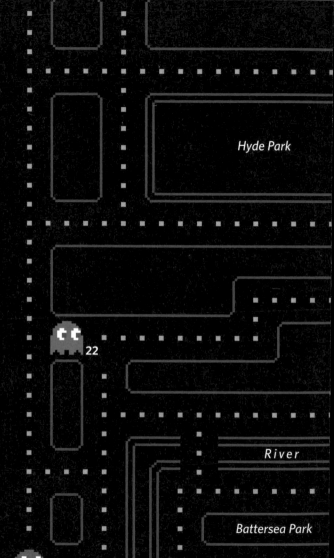

22 Brompton Cemetery
A phantom squirrel is often heard scrabbling around the northern end of the Colonnades.

23 Elephant and Castle
The tube station is haunted by ghostly girls.

24 Fulham Palace
The Great Hall of this ancient building echoes with the sound of persecuted Protestants.

25 Burgess Park
The sounds of ghostly children playing on boats can be heard along the old Surrey Canal.

26 Queen's House
One of the most famous ghost photos ever captured depicts a shrouded figure on the Tulip staircase.

 Pubs

 Transport

Houses & theatres

Parks & streets

Hyde Park

River

Battersea Park

3

8

10

11

4

5 6

7 9

Apples & Pears
cocktail bar

Millennium Mills
Site of the
world's largest
Pac-Man game:
2,219 m²

CITY OF LONDON

15

17

16

12

13 14

20

18

River Thames

21

19

SOUTH BANK

Borough
Market

ISLE
OF
DOGS

WESTMINSTER

23

FACT OR FICTION?
If you find ghost stories
hard to believe – especially
ones that involve phantom
dolphins, trees and buses –
you're right to be dubious.
Of these twenty-six tales,
one is made up. Can you
guess which one?

Thames

25

26

West London: 120 Years Later

The city has changed as much as the way we map it.

Once meticulous and highly skilled draftsmen using paper and ink, cartographers now map London with complex spatial databases of contemporary building geometry to centimetre accuracy. By overlaying this modern map form over its corresponding area from the late 19th-century Ordnance Survey One-Inch series, we can see the westward expansion of the capital. Gradually, houses and streets filled in the fields between the trunk roads built to trade with the historic city centre on the north of the Thames. Development reached its peak in the first half of the 20th century as the population boomed. London's appetite for growth persists, this time to the east where city planners are converting industrial areas into housing and parkland.

AREA ENLARGED

Development since 1895

- Buildings
- Motorways
- Primary roads
- Major roads
- Railways
- Airport runways

0   1 km

Much of London's growth has used existing development as its template. Perhaps the greatest exception to this was the construction of Heathrow Airport. The hamlet of Heathrow with its farmsteads and market gardens was paved over to make way for one of the world's busiest airports (see pp. 40–41).

SOURCES: THE NATIONAL LIBRARY OF SCOTLAND (1892-1908 MAP); KIRIL STANILOV, UNIVERSITY OF CAMBRIDGE (1895 DATA); OS (2014 BUILDINGS)

Back from The Blitz

A new East London has risen from the rubble of 'Black Saturday'.

When Hitler's *Luftwaffe* began bombing London on 7 September 1940, they set their sights on the Docklands. The plan: disable the docks – and supply chain hubs like Beckton Gas Works and the Royal Arsenal – disable a nation. The 'lightning strike' lasted 57 days, killed 430, wounded 1,600 and left the East End ablaze. Fast-forward seven decades. The port has moved downriver (see pp. 120–121). In its stead, shops, flats, parks and skyscrapers abound. Here we contrast areas damaged during the Blitz's first twenty-four hours (yellow) with the city we know today.

1 *5:50 p.m.*
Frances Street, Woolwich
DAMAGE HM War Dept.
Military College of Science
NOW Barracks

2 *5:59 p.m.*
Milborne Street, Hackney
DAMAGE Workrooms,
offices and store of a slipper
manufacturer
NOW Medium block of flats

3 *6:01 p.m.*
Well Street, Hackney
DAMAGE Both decks of
passenger bus No. EXV 246
NOW Parade of shops

4 *6:02 p.m.*
**St. Catherine's Church,
Lewisham**
DAMAGE Fire consumes the
nave and roof
NOW Church

5 *6:10 p.m.*
Stebondale St, Cubitt Town
DAMAGE 39 six-room houses
and four shops
NOW Recreation ground

6 *6:14 p.m.*
Glengall Grove, Millwall
DAMAGE The store at Walter
Voss and Co. Manufacturing
Chemists laboratories
NOW Low rise flats

7 *6:24 p.m.*
Cable Street, Stepney
DAMAGE Confectionery and
fancy goods buildings
NOW Cable Street Studios

8 *7:25 p.m.*
Union Road, Millwall
DAMAGE Machine rooms,
workshops, offices, and store
at a beer retailer
NOW Medium block of flats

9 *8:56 p.m.*
Bessemer Road, Camberwell
DAMAGE Entrance, casualty
ward of Kings College Hospital
NOW Hospital

10 *9:10 p.m.*
Hillside Road, Tulse Hill
DAMAGE Tennis net at the
Artizans Company, builder of
working-class housing
NOW Tennis courts

11 *11:59 p.m.*
Benledi Street, Poplar
DAMAGE 57 buildings;
Fire Brigade rescues four
severely injured people
NOW Flats, park

12 *12:44 a.m.*
Old Kent Road, Southwark
DAMAGE Four seats at the
Astoria, an Art Deco cinema
NOW Parade of shops

SOURCES: NATIONAL ARCHIVES; GUARDIAN DATASTORE

Queen
Elizabeth
Olympic
Park

Victoria
Park

2
3

East India
Docks

11

Beckton
Gas Works

St Paul's
Cathedral

London
Docks

7

West India
Docks

Royal Victoria Dock

Royal Albert Dock
London City Airport
King George V Dock

City Hall

Surrey
Commercial
Docks

Canary Wharf

O₂
Arena

River   Thames

Royal
Arsenal

London Eye

Westminster
Abbey

Southwark
Park

8

6

Millwall
Docks

5

1

Burgess Park

12

Greenwich
Park

Woolwich
Common

9

4

Oxleas
Wood

Brockwell
Park

Peckham Rye
Common

Dulwich
Park

10

6 3

Central line
cross-section shown
to the right

Roding
Valley

Grange
Hill

West Ruislip

Ealing Broadway

Bond
Street

The 2012 Olympics
increased rents to the east
of the Central Line as people
clamoured to be close to
the action. Now that the
athletes' village has been
converted to flats, supply is
closer to matching demand,
so rents there have fallen.

0   5 km

**Change in median
monthly rent (£)**
January to April, 2013–14

INCREASE

101–1,200 more

51–100

21–50

11–20

9 less–10 more

10–19

20–49

50–99

100–653 less

DECREASE

Generation Rent

London has become a city of renters.

London has so much to offer that people the world over are looking to bed down wherever they can. With such huge demand, prices are rising. Here we show where average rents for two-bedroom flats have increased (or decreased) between 2013 and 2014. After tax, the median income for those in London is about £500 per week, so for those at the limits of what they can afford, a small increase can make a big difference. It's not all bad news though. Some areas are getting cheaper (9%). And thanks to ever more sophisticated property search engines, it's never been easier to seek out a bargain.

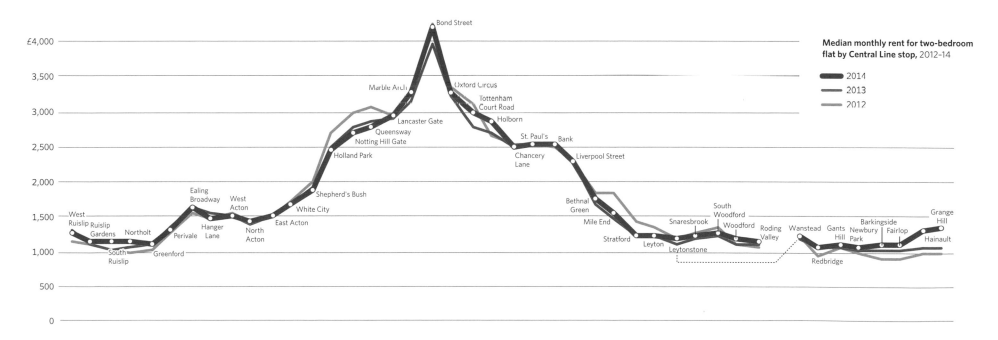

Median monthly rent for two-bedroom flat by Central Line stop, 2012-14

— 2014
— 2013
— 2012

SOURCE: NESTORIA.CO.UK

ENFIELD

Central line
cross-section shown
to the right

BARNET

Roding
Valley

Grange
Hill

HARROW

HARINGEY

WALTHAM
FOREST

HAVERING

West Ruislip

BRENT

HACKNEY

REDBRIDGE

EALING

CAMDEN

ISLINGTON

NEWHAM

BARKING
& DAGENHAM

HILLINGDON

Ealing
Broadway

HAMMERSMITH & FULHAM

KENSINGTON & CHELSEA

WESTMINSTER

CITY

TOWER
HAMLETS

Marble
Arch

GREENWICH

HOUNSLOW

SOUTHWARK

BEXLEY

RICHMOND
UPON THAMES

WANDSWORTH

LAMBETH

LEWISHAM

MERTON

KINGSTON
UPON
THAMES

0   5 km

CROYDON

SUTTON

BROMLEY

Median flat price (£)
May 2014

250,000

200,000

150,000

100,000

85,000

No properties sold for
less than £250,000

£2.5 million

If both members of a couple have
median London salaries and have
been able to save their mortgage
deposit – or can withdraw it from
'the bank of Mum and Dad' – then
spending £250,000 on a first flat
would be reasonable. This is half
the average house price in London
(as of January 2014) and the
same as the UK average.

(Un)Affordable Flats

When it comes to property, only the wealthy are burning a hole in their pockets.

London has more billionaires than any other city, so not everyone is concerned about the cost of housing. Nearly 500 flats sold for over £2.5 million in 2013 alone. This map shows what is left for the rest of us.

Central living is out of the question. As price increases spread like wildfire across the capital, only smaller and more fractured areas of affordability remain. With global demand fanning the flames, there is little more Londoners can do than to stick it out as 'Generation Rent' or move to one of the stars in London's constellation of commuter towns (see pp. 42–3).

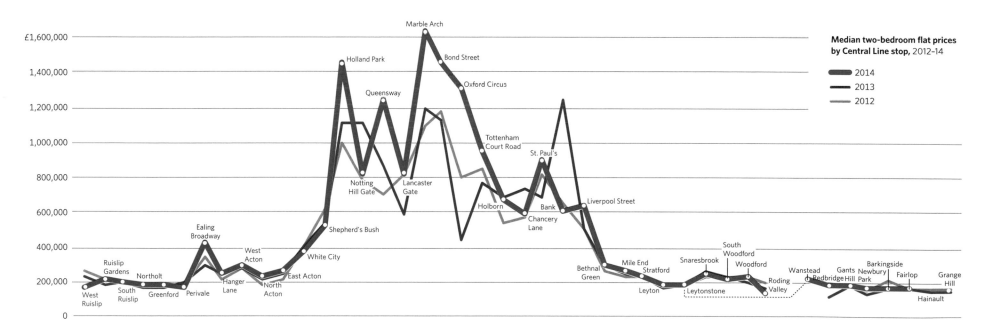

Median two-bedroom flat prices by Central Line stop, 2012–14

— 2014
— 2013
— 2012

13 Views
Worth Protecting

Will the skyline of the future honour its past?

It started with a Gherkin. Then the Cheesegrater, the Walkie-Talkie and the Shard. Now there's talk of 230 new skyscrapers with names like The Blades, The Stage and The Quill. Many Londoners fear these new towers – especially those funded by foreign investors – will eclipse their ancestors: the Palace of Westminster and St Paul's Cathedral. Fortunately, the London Plan has identified 27 cherished views, including thirteen 'Protected Vistas' that cannot be obstructed. We visited all of them and recorded what we saw in case things don't go according to plan.

Protected Vistas
2014

⑥ Alexandra Palace
Kenwood House ⑦
⑧ ⑩
Parliament Hill ⑨
⑪
Primrose Hill ⑫
St Paul's Cathedral
Serpentine Bridge ③
Tower of London
① ④
Palace of Westminster
⑤ ② Blackheath Point
Greenwich Park
⑬ King Henry's Mound

① St Paul's from Westminster Pier

The London Plan protects four types of view: panoramas (2, 5), river prospects, linear views and townscapes. Linear views like the one from Westminster Pier (1) frame landmarks in a 'keyhole'. Townscapes celebrate classic vantages like Serpentine Bridge (3) and Queen's Walk (4).

② St Paul's from Greenwich Park

⑤ St Paul's from Blackheath Point

③ Westminster from Serpentine Bridge

④ Tower of London from Queen's Walk

(6) St Paul's from Alexandra Palace

(7) St Paul's from Kenwood House

(8) St Paul's from Parliament Hill

(10) St Paul's from Hampstead Heath

These seven panoramas look south towards Central London and include either the Palace of Westminster or St Paul's Cathedral. Notice how The Shard photobombs St Paul's. Residents in Hampstead sure do.

(11) St Paul's from Primrose Hill

THE ORIGINAL 'KEYHOLE'

⑬ St Paul's from King Henry's Mound

⑨ Westminster from Parliament Hill

⑫ Westminster from Primrose Hill

2 WHO WE ARE

DNA of the City

Census variables reveal London's genetic code.

The 2011 Census questionnaire for England contained fifty-six questions that solicited a broad spectrum of answers. Multiply these by 3.27 million households in London and that's a lot of data for one city. It took the Office for National Statistics (ONS) the best part of two years to release headline figures, covering the likes of gender, religion, ethnicity and employment. To convey the magnitude of their task, we have taken 207 variables from 16 of these categories and shown their values in all 649 London wards, grouped here by borough. Instead of numbers, we used colours. More intense colours correspond to higher values and reveal areas with, for example, more Buddhists than another. 134,343 blocks may seem like a lot, but it's only a fraction of the data collected. To include everything would require a plot 305 times this size, large enough to fill the floor of a Tube carriage!

SOURCE: 2011 CENSUS, ONS

Country of Birth | Passports Held | Religion | Health | Communal Housing Residents | Qualifications & Students | Economic Activity | Hours | Industry | Occupation | Socio-Economic Class

(1) Older Londoners tend to live in outer boroughs like Havering for a quieter life away from the city centre.

(2) Singles call London's inner boroughs home; marriage prompts a move to outer areas. See pp. 84–5.

(3) Tower Hamlets is known for its large Bangladeshi community. Other migrants live there too. See pp. 102–3.

(4) The greatest number of Londoners with no or an unstated religion live in Camden and Islington.

(5) Wards such as Knightsbridge and Belgravia, Marylebone High Street and Lancaster Gate have some of the highest numbers of people in the top tier of the ONS's socio-economic classification, those working as high-level managers.

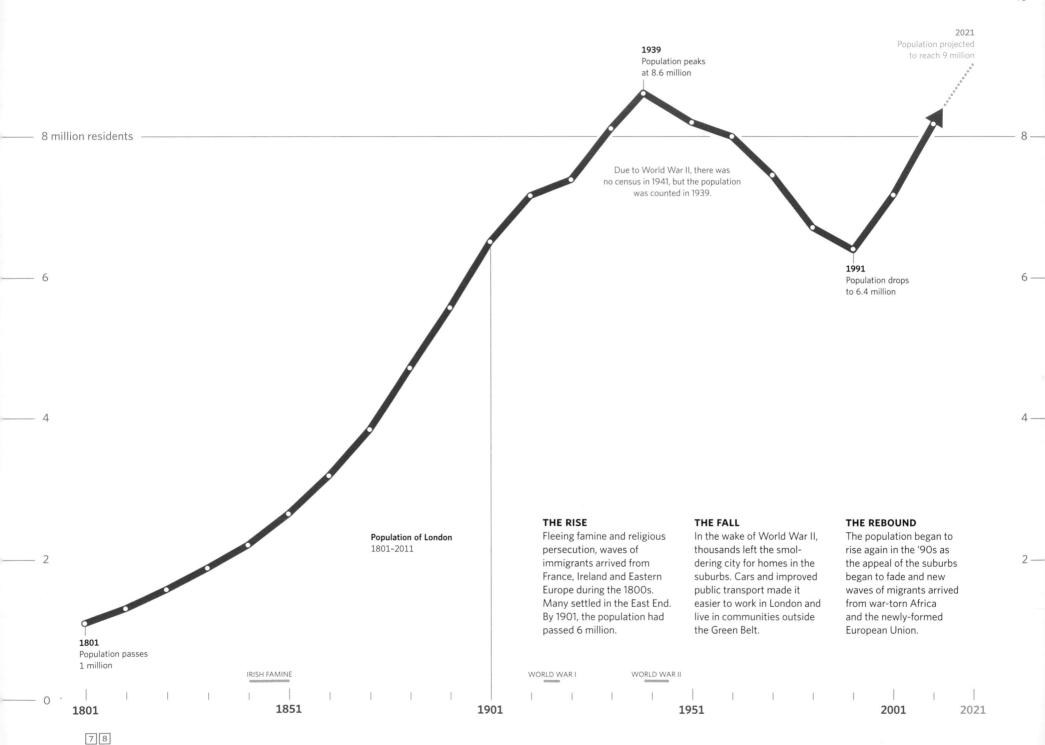

Population of London
1801–2011

10
10

8 million residents
8

6
6

4
4

2
2

0

1801 **1851** **1901** **1951** **2001** 2021

IRISH FAMINE   WORLD WAR I   WORLD WAR II

1801
Population passes
1 million

1939
Population peaks
at 8.6 million

Due to World War II, there was
no census in 1941, but the population
was counted in 1939.

2021
Population projected
to reach 9 million

1991
Population drops
to 6.4 million

THE RISE
Fleeing famine and religious
persecution, waves of
immigrants arrived from
France, Ireland and Eastern
Europe during the 1800s.
Many settled in the East End.
By 1901, the population had
passed 6 million.

THE FALL
In the wake of World War II,
thousands left the smol-
dering city for homes in the
suburbs. Cars and improved
public transport made it
easier to work in London and
live in communities outside
the Green Belt.

THE REBOUND
The population began to
rise again in the '90s as
the appeal of the suburbs
began to fade and new
waves of migrants arrived
from war-torn Africa
and the newly-formed
European Union.

Why it's worth knowing who we are

For statisticians, Sunday 27 March 2011 was a big day. Across the UK, regardless of age, sex, income, religion or politics, households filled out census forms – answering 56 questions such as 'Who usually lives here?' and 'How many hours a week do you usually work?' – and posted them back to the Office for National Statistics (ONS). The result? The latest snapshot in a series that plays back 210 years of UK history like a stop-motion movie.

It takes minutes to fill out the census form but years for ONS to fully process and share the data collected. Like a trailer for a long-anticipated film, the first data from this national event were released in July 2012. In a decade, the population of England and Wales had grown 7.1% to 56.1 million – the most rapid increase in the history of the census. In London, growth was faster – up 12% to 8.2 million. With each subsequent data release, life in London could be seen in ever-higher definition from the passports people hold to the jobs they work.

The problem is, gathering high-quality data costs money: £482 million to be exact for the 2011 Census. With cost savings in mind, the UK's new Conservative-led coalition government questioned the census's value to tax payers. They first explored the option of cancelling it but then reconsidered. We are fortunate they did because, as the Royal Statistical Society put it, census data ensure 'that we build our schools where they are required by our children, that hospitals are equipped to deliver the services that we need, that transport links reflect the journeys we undertake. With good data we can get these things right (and can hold people to account should things go wrong).'

The biggest limitation of the census is its infrequency. A wealth of new technologies offer near-continuous supplies of data from existing government databases such as tax records or the National Health Service through to smartphones and social media. However, quantity is no substitute for quality. For example, if you were to learn that 1% of Twitter users in London tweet in Arabic, you still wouldn't know how many Londoners speak Arabic. To appear on our 'Twitter Ink' map (pp. 106–107), you needed a smartphone *and* you needed to be tweeting. It's a self-selected sample. To be included in the census, all you need is a pen and a post-box.

The census is our control. It provides the baseline to see how accurately experimental data sources can answer questions like 'Where do most of London's Arabic speakers live?' or 'How many people moved to London last year?' If we get it right, we'll be able to monitor change almost hourly as population statistics transition from static to streaming. Get it wrong and we won't really know who we are until the next census in 2021.

Similarities Attract

We are where we live.

To better understand the demographic diversity of London, the Greater London Authority (GLA) asked geographers Paul Longley and Alex Singleton to map it. This is no easy task. As the previous pages show, Londoners span the full spectrum of ethnicities, ages and occupations. Their infinite combinations don't readily fit into typical classifications. So first, Longley and Singleton ran variables from the 2011 Census through a clustering algorithm to identify eight broad groups of people with similar population and built environment characteristics (e.g. White, homeowners, students). Then they ran it again within each of those groups to get more specific. The resulting kaleidoscope (right) helps the city target local initiatives and tells new businesses where to set up shop.

AREA ENLARGED

Neighbourhood classifications, 2014
Each colour encapsulates a combination of census variables.
These are the official categories approved by the GLA.

Urban elites
- Educational advantage
- City central

City vibe
- City and student fringe
- Graduation occupation

London life-cycle
- City enclaves
- Affluent suburbs

Settled Asians
- Asian owner occupiers
- Transport service workers
- East End Asians
- Elderly Asians

High density and high-rise flats
- Students and minority mix
- Disadvantaged diaspora
- Bangladeshi enclaves

Multi-ethnic suburbs
- Affordable transitions
- Public sector and service employees

Intermediate lifestyles
- Struggling suburbs
- Suburban localities

Ageing city fringe
- Detached retirement
- Not quite Home Counties

SOURCES: 2011 CENSUS, ONS; PAUL LONGLEY, UNIVERSITY COLLEGE LONDON AND ALEX SINGLETON, UNIVERSITY OF LIVERPOOL

BRENT

EALING

HOUNSLOW

BARNET

HARINGEY

WALTHAM
FOREST

REDBRIDGE

*Hampstead
Heath*

CAMDEN

ISLINGTON

HACKNEY

*Victoria
Park*

NEWHAM

*Regent's
Park*

WESTMINSTER

CITY

TOWER HAMLETS

Hyde Park

River Thames

KENSINGTON
& CHELSEA

*Battersea
Park*

SOUTHWARK

*Greenwich
Park*

HAMMERSMITH
& FULHAM

GREENWICH

LAMBETH

*Richmond
Park*

WANDSWORTH

LEWISHAM

MERTON

0   1 km

Life and Death

Only one explanation adds up.

London's population increased by 100,000 in 2012. Everyone wants to know why. There are four possible causes: more migrants from within the UK, more from overseas, more babies or fewer deaths. As we explain later in this chapter, internal migration (pp. 94–5) and international migration (pp. 96–7) directly accounted for a net increase of only 14,000 people, which means the city's unchecked growth is a matter of life or death. We'll give you a hint: it's not death. In fact, the causes overlap somewhat. Births outnumbered deaths 134,000 to 48,000 but more than half of those babies belonged to mothers born outside the UK. If total births in London continue to increase by 2,500 per year, the population will hit nine million in the next decade.

In these graphics, we show how the fertility and mortality rates for each borough compared to the London average over a ten-year span. Women in Inner London are having fewer babies than those in Outer London, where Barking & Dagenham had the highest fertility rate of all.

READ CLOCKWISE
2003 → 2012

AMOUNT ABOVE OR BELOW THE LONDON AVERAGE

Fertility rate by borough
2003–2012

ONS MEASURES FERTILITY BY THE NUMBER OF LIVE BIRTHS PER 1,000 WOMEN AGED 15-44.

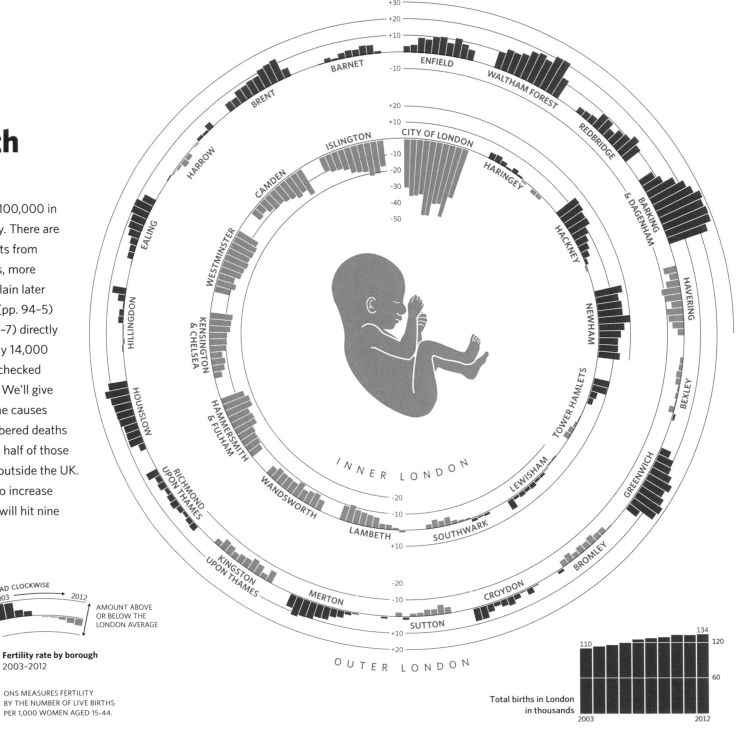

Total births in London in thousands

+20
+10
ENFIELD
BARNET
-10
-20
WALTHAM FOREST
BRENT
REDBRIDGE
+20
+10
HARROW
CITY OF LONDON
-10
ISLINGTON
-20
BARKING & DAGENHAM
CAMDEN
-30
HARINGEY
EALING
-40
-50
HACKNEY
HAVERING
WESTMINSTER
HILLINGDON
NEWHAM
KENSINGTON & CHELSEA
BEXLEY
HOUNSLOW
TOWER HAMLETS
HAMMERSMITH & FULHAM
GREENWICH
WANDSWORTH
RICHMOND UPON THAMES
INNER LONDON
LEWISHAM
LAMBETH
-20
SOUTHWARK
-10
KINGSTON UPON THAMES
+20
BROMLEY
MERTON
CROYDON
-20
-10
SUTTON
+10
+20
OUTER LONDON

READ CLOCKWISE
2003 → 2012
AMOUNT ABOVE
OR BELOW THE
LONDON AVERAGE

Mortality rate by borough
2003–2012

ONS MEASURES MORTALITY BY DIVIDING
OBSERVED DEATHS BY THE NUMBER EXPECTED
BASED ON THE AGE OF AN AREA'S POPULATION.

58   48
Total deaths in London
in thousands
2003   2012

Deaths have been delayed
in wealthier boroughs like
Kensington & Chelsea and
Richmond upon Thames where
residents can afford healthier
lifestyles. Not so in eastern
boroughs like Tower Hamlets
where there have been far
more deaths than expected.

Relationship Status

We age, we marry, we migrate.

Twenty-five and single? In London, you're anything but alone. According to the 2011 Census, more than half of twentysomethings go solo. Then come your thirties and that deep river of available singles your age narrows to a shallow stream. By age fifty, it's little more than a trickle.

Most will have married and settled in the leafier boroughs (see maps). Young singles – and their cohabiting friends – prefer trendier parts of the city such as Hoxton, Clapham and Peckham. Those living away from their spouse fall into two camps: pricey places in Kensington or more affordable housing near Heathrow, Wembley and Upton Park. Separated couples and divorcees cluster around Tottenham and to the east; widowed spouses stay put.

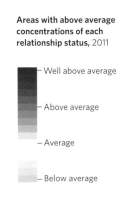

Areas with above average concentrations of each relationship status, 2011

- Well above average
- Above average
- Average
- Below average

SINGLE — **31.7**% of Londoners

COHABITING — **11.4**%

MARRIED — **39.6**%

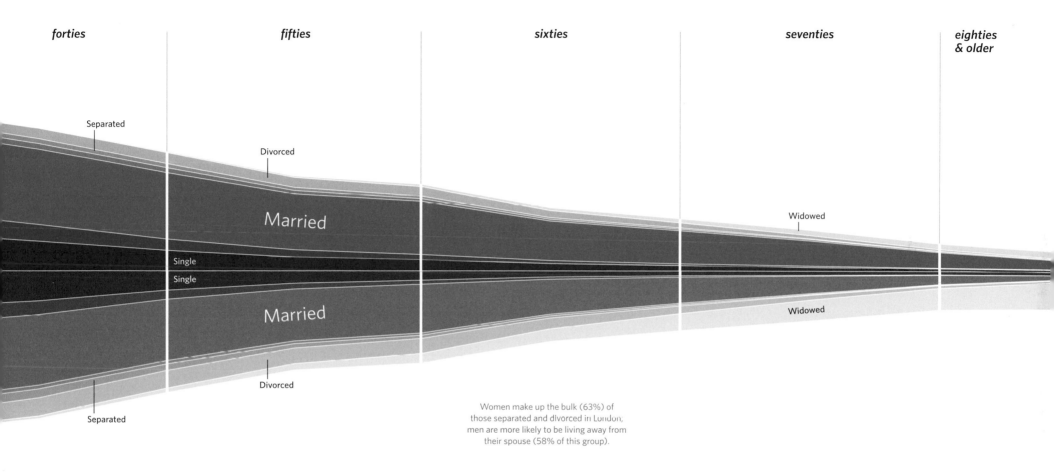

forties | *fifties* | *sixties* | *seventies* | *eighties & older*

Separated

Divorced

Married

Widowed

Single

Single

Married

Widowed

Divorced

Separated

Women make up the bulk (63%) of
those separated and divorced in London;
men are more likely to be living away from
their spouse (58% of this group).

MARRIED BUT LIVING APART   **3.1**%

Wembley

Upton Park

Kensington

Heathrow

Croydon

SEPARATED   **2.8**%

Tottenham

Wembley   Ilford

New Cross

DIVORCED   **6.4**%

Tottenham

WIDOWED   **5**%

Uxbridge

Upminster

Bromley

SOURCES: 2011 CENSUS, ONS; OS

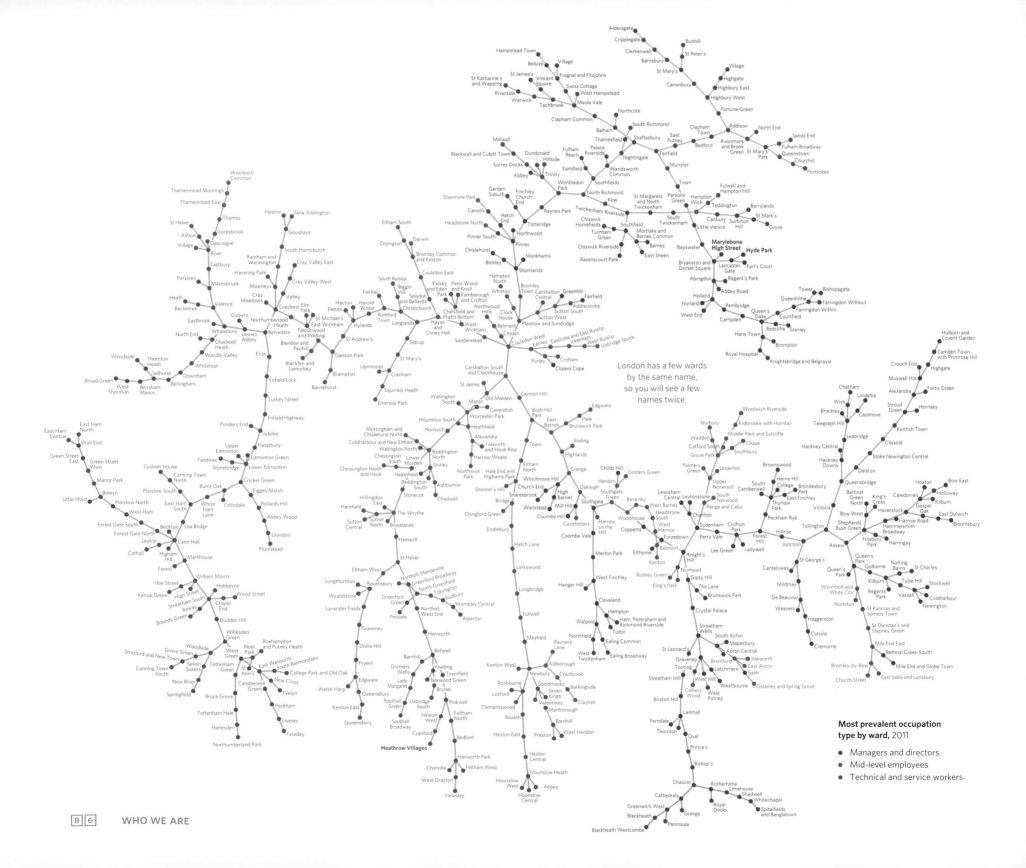

London has a few wards
by the same name,
so you will see a few
names twice.

**Most prevalent occupation
type by ward,** 2011

- Managers and directors
- Mid-level employees
- Technical and service workers

Professional Networking

It's not what you know but where you live.

Imagine London as one big company and within it, the twenty-four occupation types registered in the 2011 Census from corporate managers to machine operatives. The tree to the left then is an organizational chart, grouping areas together that have similar concentrations of workers in those twenty-four job types. Blue areas have lots of degree-level managers and directors; green areas have lots of mid-level employees; and brown areas have lots of technical and service workers. Much like at an office (or on LinkedIn), those connected to each other share the most in common.

The algorithm we used to generate this network did not factor in geography, only job types from the 2011 Census. Still, some adjacent areas on the map (below right) remain adjacent on this tree. That's because socio-economic classes tend to stick together. For example, Hyde Park and Marylebone High Street wards both have 15% of their residents working as corporate managers. Contrast those areas with Heathrow Villages. With 20% working in technical and service jobs, they're not just on opposite ends of the city. They're on opposite ends of the ladder.

On this tree, some nodes differ in colour from the rest of their branch. These areas may be changing, thereby transitioning them from one set of employment characteristics to another.

Here we transfer the colours from the network tree to the true geography of London's 649 wards. This reveals the concentration of managers and directors (blue) in Central London.

SOURCE: 2011 CENSUS, ONS

There's a Guild for That

Art scholars and educators join the butchers, bakers and candlestick makers.

A thousand years before smartphones, Londoners turned to craftsmen to get things done. Fletchers fletched arrows, Grocers sold spices 'in gross', and Cordwainers worked – or 'wained' – leather from Cordoba. Gradually they formed guilds, which began as religious, commercial or social associations in different parts of the City. Streets like Cloth Fair and Ironmonger Lane still recall the guilds, which came to be known as livery companies for the bicoloured garments – or livery – worn by members and servants. Here we have redesigned the coat of arms for all 110 'Worshipful Companies' as app icons. They are arranged by their order of precedence (see note), beginning with the 'Great Twelve'.

Early companies like the Bonnet Makers and Heaumers vanished with their trades; others like the Horners and Fanmakers adapted their crafts to plastics and air conditioning respectively, or shifted their focus to charitable giving. After the Fanmakers in 1709, no new companies were established until the 1920s, when the Master Mariners and Air Pilots and Air Navigators became the first of the thirty-three 'modern livery companies', a group that now includes trades of today: Educators, International Bankers and Information Technologists.

THE GREAT TWELVE

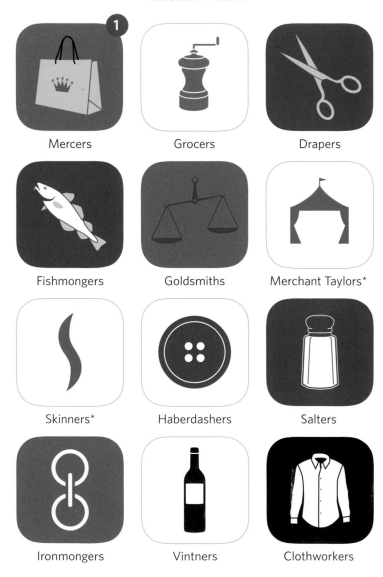

Mercers Grocers Drapers

Fishmongers Goldsmiths Merchant Taylors*

Skinners* Haberdashers Salters

Ironmongers Vintners Clothworkers

*In the 15th century, the Skinners and Merchant Taylors both claimed to deserve sixth place in the order of precedence. To settle this dispute, the Lord Mayor decreed in 1484 that the two companies would alternate between sixth and seventh every year, and they have ever since.

Dyers
 Brewers
 Leathersellers
 Pewterers
 Barbers
 Cutlers
 Bakers
 Wax Chandlers
 Tallow Chandlers

Dyers · Brewers · Leathersellers · Pewterers · Barbers · Cutlers · Bakers · Wax Chandlers · Tallow Chandlers

 Armourers & Brasiers
 Girdlers
 Butchers
 Saddlers
 Carpenters
 Cordwainers
 Painter-Stainers
 Curriers
 Masons

Armourers & Brasiers · Girdlers · Butchers · Saddlers · Carpenters · Cordwainers · Painter-Stainers · Curriers · Masons

 Plumbers
 Innholders
 Founders
 Poulters
 Cooks
 Coopers
 Tylers & Bricklayers
 Bowyers
 Fletchers

Plumbers · Innholders · Founders · Poulters · Cooks · Coopers · Tylers & Bricklayers · Bowyers · Fletchers

 Blacksmiths
 Joiners & Ceilers
 Weavers**
 Woolmen
 Scriveners
 Fruiterers
 Plaisterers
 Stationers & Newspaper Makers
 Broderers

Blacksmiths · Joiners & Ceilers · Weavers** · Woolmen · Scriveners · Fruiterers · Plaisterers · Stationers & Newspaper Makers · Broderers

ORDER OF PRECEDENCE
The City assigns each new company a position in the order of precedence. The order for the first 48 was 'sette, ordeyned, and agreed' by the Court of Aldermen in 1515 according to each company's wealth and influence at that time. All subsequent companies have been numbered consecutively, from the Upholders (49) to the Art Scholars (110), who attained livery status in February 2014.

 Upholders
 Musicians
 Turners
 Basketmakers
 Glaziers
 Horners
 Farriers
 Paviors
 Loriners
 Apothecaries
 Shipwrights
 Spectacle Makers
 Clockmakers
 Glovers
 Feltmakers

Upholders · Musicians · Turners · Basketmakers · Glaziers · Horners · Farriers · Paviors · Loriners · Apothecaries · Shipwrights · Spectacle Makers · Clockmakers · Glovers · Feltmakers

** The Weavers' charter dates to 1155, making them the oldest chartered craft in the City.

 Framework Knitters
 Needle Makers
 Gardeners
 Tin Plate Workers
 Wheelwrights
 Distillers
 Patten Makers
 Glass Sellers
 Coachmakers
 Gunmakers
 Silver Wyre Drawers
 Makers of Playing Cards
 Fanmakers
 Carmen
 Master Mariners

Framework Knitters · Needle Makers · Gardeners · Tin Plate Workers · Wheelwrights · Distillers · Patten Makers · Glass Sellers · Coachmakers · Gunmakers · Silver Wyre Drawers · Makers of Playing Cards · Fanmakers · Carmen · Master Mariners

 Solicitors
 Farmers
 Air Pilots & Air Navigators
 Tobacco Blenders
 Furniture Makers
 Scientific Inst. Makers
 Chartered Surveyors
 Chartered Accountants
 Chartered Secretaries
 Builders' Merchants
 Launderers
 Marketors
 Actuaries
 Insurers
 Arbitrators
 Engineers

Solicitors · Farmers · Air Pilots & Air Navigators · Tobacco Blenders · Furniture Makers · Scientific Inst. Makers · Chartered Surveyors · Chartered Accountants · Chartered Secretaries · Builders' Merchants · Launderers · Marketors · Actuaries · Insurers · Arbitrators · Engineers

 Fuellers
 Lightmongers
 Enviro. Cleaners
 Chartered Architects
 Constructors
 Information Technologists
 World Traders
 Water Conservators
 Firefighters
 Carriage Drivers
 Management Consultants
 Intl. Bankers
 Tax Advisers
 Security Professionals
 Educators
 Art Scholars

Fuellers · Lightmongers · Enviro. Cleaners · Chartered Architects · Constructors · Information Technologists · World Traders · Water Conservators · Firefighters · Carriage Drivers · Management Consultants · Intl. Bankers · Tax Advisers · Security Professionals · Educators · Art Scholars

SOURCES: *DISCOVERING LONDON'S GUILDS AND LIVERIES* BY JOHN KENNEDY MELLING; CITY OF LONDON

Fifty Kilometres of Jobs

A chain of high streets unites London's villages.

Shoes, jewellery, coffee, halal meats and fried chicken. Hair stylists, optometrists and immigration lawyers. Hospitals, mosques and pubs. You can find them all along Whitechapel Road in Tower Hamlets (below). Nearly 600 of these corridors line the capital. Here we show how many link together to form a chain from Uxbridge to Romford with the world's most famous, Oxford Street, at its centre. Often thought of as places of leisure, high streets double up to provide office space on their upper floors. The coloured bars below show the estimated numbers of floors available for employment; colour indicates the usage type.

Romford

Uxbridge

ENLARGED
BELOW

GREATER LONDON
AUTHORITY
BOUNDARY

Uxbridge

Hillingdon

Southall

Ealing

Acton

Shepherd's Bush

Notting Hill

Hyde Park

Kilometre 1
BUSINESSES 146
FLOORS 1,535

Kilometre 9
BUSINESSES 238
FLOORS 1,005

Kilometre 14
BUSINESSES 240
FLOORS 5,195

Kilometre 50
BUSINESSES 129
FLOORS 597

Kilometre 37
BUSINESSES 301
FLOORS 2,100

**Estimated number of floors
by business type,** July 2010

— Shop
— Business & finance
— Food & drink
— Industry & storage
— Hotel
— Institution
— Assembly

It's easy to focus
on London's 'retail
centres' at the heart of
its villages and forget
the shops along the
roads that link them.
The purpose of this
survey was to remind
planners of their
importance.

Kilometre 27
BUSINESSES 307
FLOORS 7,935

Kilometre 31
BUSINESSES 225
FLOORS 3,125

SOURCE: GORT SCOTT ARCHITECTS. PHOTO COLLAGE: JULIAN HARRAP ARCHITECTS LLP

Votes by political party,
May 2014

Labour

Conservative   Other

2014

On these maps, 'Other'
includes parties on the left
and right as well as independent candidates. The greens
in Southwark are Liberal
Democrat voters, whereas
just across the Thames they
are voters for the local party
Tower Hamlets First.

The Colour of Votes

Red is rising in London's political mix.

When it comes to voting in London, things are far
from black and white. The ballots for the May 2014
council elections featured more than twenty parties.
To the left we show the results for Labour (red),
Conservative (blue) and everyone else (green),
including British National Party, Christian People's
Alliance and the Trade Unionist and Socialist
Coalition. For example, a very well-organized group
of independent councillors from local residents'
groups has kept the Borough of Havering coloured
green for three straight elections (see right). Over the
past few years, greens have turned to red as liberal
Londoners have switched from Liberal Democrats to
Labour in response to national issues that made the
party less popular. The Conservative voters in Westminster and Kensington and Chelsea seem a more
loyal bunch, keeping the red at bay.

2006

Support for the Labour party
and its London Mayor Ken
Livingstone was beginning
to wane as Londoners were
becoming more enamored
with the Boris Johnson, the
soon-to-be-elected Conservative mayor.

2010

Conservatives edged Labour
nationally and locally and
formed a coalition government
with Liberal Democrats. Votes
for the far right-wing British
National Party peak in Barking
and Dagenham in an area of
traditional Labour supporters.

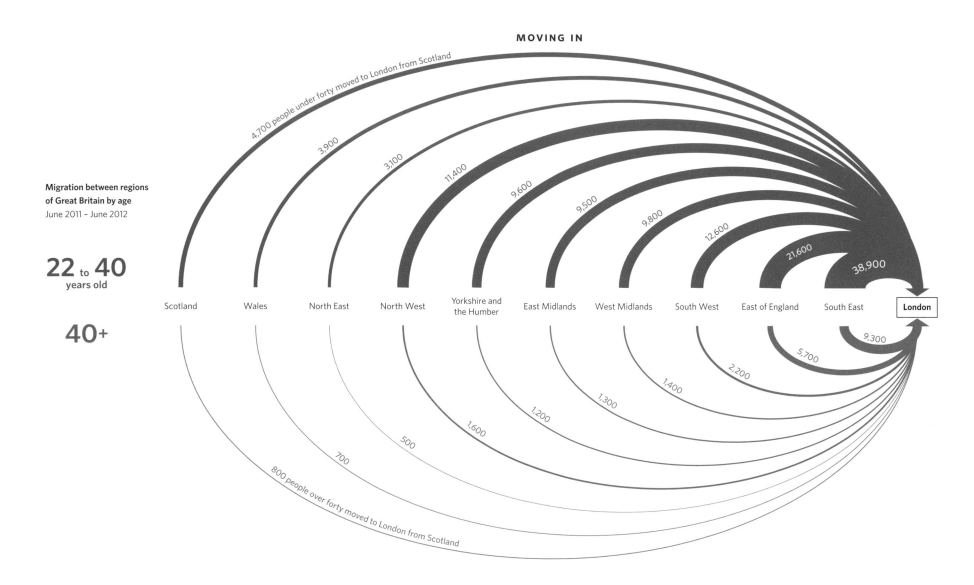

Migration between regions of Great Britain by age
June 2011 – June 2012

22 to 40 years old

40+

4,700 people under forty moved to London from Scotland

3,900

3,100

11,400

9,600

9,500

9,800

12,600

21,600

38,900

Scotland | Wales | North East | North West | Yorkshire and the Humber | East Midlands | West Midlands | South West | East of England | South East | London

9,300

5,700

2,200

1,400

1,300

1,200

1,600

500

700

800 people over forty moved to London from Scotland

Moving In, Then On

London's population may be growing, but not everyone is sticking around.

Unlike parcels in the post, people have no tracking numbers to record their movements around the country. Instead, the Office for National Statistics (ONS) creates estimates by combining higher education records with patient register data. If a person registers with a new doctor in a new region, that counts as a move. Across all age groups, between 2011 and 2012, London experienced the largest turnover margin in the country: 55,000 more people left than arrived. Looking at those aged 22 or older, the arcs above show

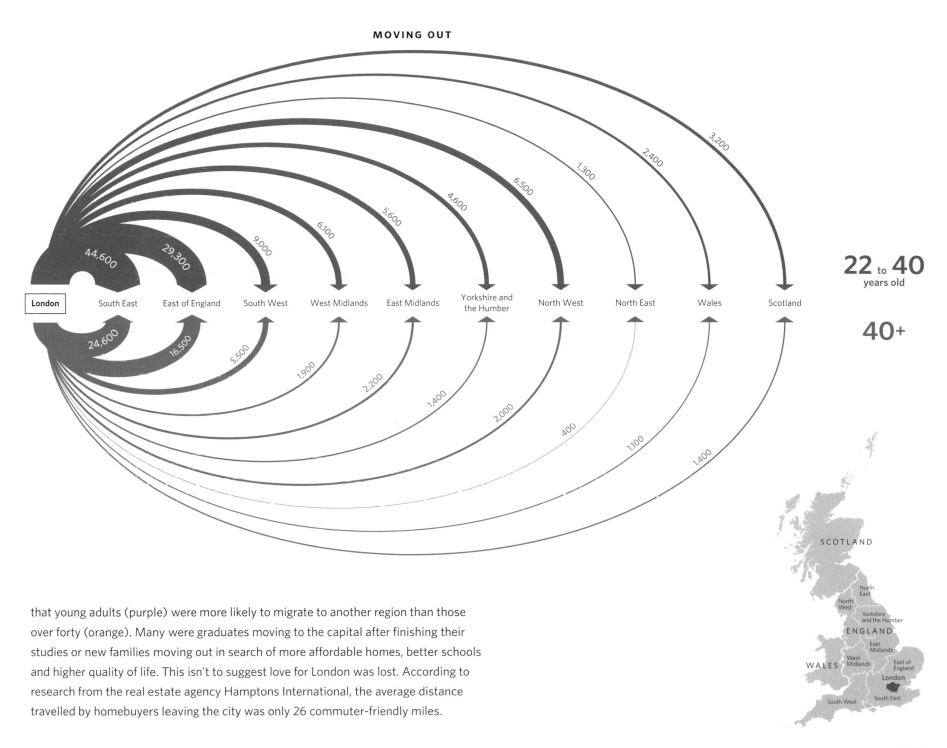

MOVING OUT

44,600
29,300
9,000
6,100
5,600
4,600
6,500
1,300
2,400
3,200

22 to **40**
years old

40+

London   South East   East of England   South West   West Midlands   East Midlands   Yorkshire and the Humber   North West   North East   Wales   Scotland

24,600
16,500
5,500
1,900
2,200
1,400
2,000
400
1,100
1,400

SCOTLAND

North East

North West

Yorkshire and the Humber

ENGLAND

East Midlands

WALES

West Midlands

East of England

London

South East

South West

that young adults (purple) were more likely to migrate to another region than those over forty (orange). Many were graduates moving to the capital after finishing their studies or new families moving out in search of more affordable homes, better schools and higher quality of life. This isn't to suggest love for London was lost. According to research from the real estate agency Hamptons International, the average distance travelled by homebuyers leaving the city was only 26 commuter-friendly miles.

SOURCE: ONS

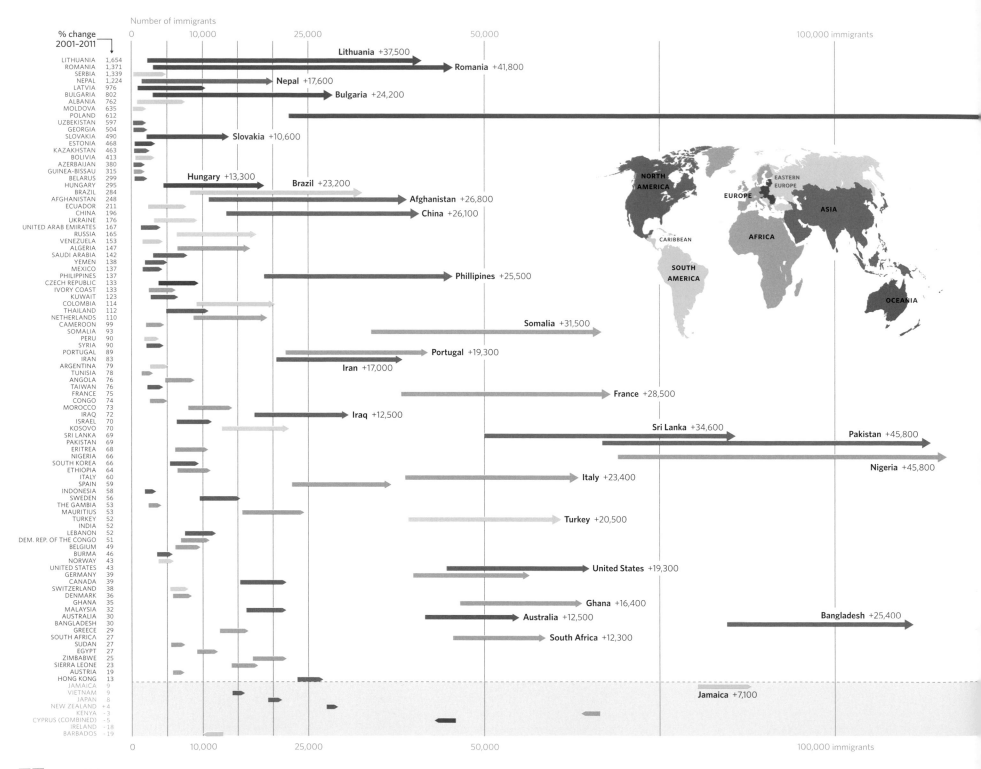

Number of immigrants

% change
2001-2011

Country	%
LITHUANIA	1,654
ROMANIA	1,371
SERBIA	1,339
NEPAL	1,224
LATVIA	976
BULGARIA	802
ALBANIA	762
MOLDOVA	635
POLAND	612
UZBEKISTAN	597
GEORGIA	504
SLOVAKIA	490
ESTONIA	468
KAZAKHSTAN	463
BOLIVIA	413
AZERBAIJAN	380
GUINEA-BISSAU	315
BELARUS	299
HUNGARY	295
BRAZIL	284
AFGHANISTAN	248
ECUADOR	211
CHINA	196
UKRAINE	176
UNITED ARAB EMIRATES	167
RUSSIA	165
VENEZUELA	153
ALGERIA	147
SAUDI ARABIA	142
YEMEN	138
MEXICO	137
PHILIPPINES	137
CZECH REPUBLIC	133
IVORY COAST	133
KUWAIT	123
COLOMBIA	114
THAILAND	112
NETHERLANDS	110
CAMEROON	99
SOMALIA	93
PERU	90
SYRIA	90
PORTUGAL	89
IRAN	83
ARGENTINA	79
TUNISIA	78
ANGOLA	76
TAIWAN	76
FRANCE	75
CONGO	74
MOROCCO	73
IRAQ	72
ISRAEL	70
KOSOVO	70
SRI LANKA	69
PAKISTAN	69
ERITREA	68
NIGERIA	66
SOUTH KOREA	66
ETHIOPIA	64
ITALY	60
SPAIN	59
INDONESIA	58
SWEDEN	56
THE GAMBIA	53
MAURITIUS	53
TURKEY	52
INDIA	52
LEBANON	52
DEM. REP. OF THE CONGO	51
BELGIUM	49
BURMA	46
NORWAY	43
UNITED STATES	43
GERMANY	39
CANADA	39
SWITZERLAND	38
DENMARK	36
GHANA	35
MALAYSIA	32
AUSTRALIA	30
BANGLADESH	30
GREECE	29
SOUTH AFRICA	27
SUDAN	27
EGYPT	27
ZIMBABWE	25
SIERRA LEONE	23
AUSTRIA	19
HONG KONG	13
JAMAICA	9
VIETNAM	9
JAPAN	8
NEW ZEALAND	+4
KENYA	-3
CYPRUS (COMBINED)	-5
IRELAND	-18
BARBADOS	-19

Lithuania +37,500
Romania +41,800
Nepal +17,600
Bulgaria +24,200
Slovakia +10,600
Hungary +13,300
Brazil +23,200
Afghanistan +26,800
China +26,100
Phillipines +25,500
Somalia +31,500
Portugal +19,300
Iran +17,000
France +28,500
Iraq +12,500
Sri Lanka +34,600
Pakistan +45,800
Nigeria +45,800
Italy +23,400
Turkey +20,500
United States +19,300
Ghana +16,400
Australia +12,500
Bangladesh +25,400
South Africa +12,300
Jamaica +7,100

NORTH AMERICA
EASTERN EUROPE
EUROPE
ASIA
CARIBBEAN
AFRICA
SOUTH AMERICA
OCEANIA

0   10,000   25,000   50,000   100,000 immigrants

Increasingly Eastern

Expanding the European Union brought a surge of new Londoners.

With this chart we show the changing numbers of migrants in London from ninety-eight countries between the 2001 and 2011 Censuses ranked by percentage change. At the top sits Lithuania, a small nation in Eastern Europe. In 2001, there were fewer than 3,000 Lithuanians living in London. By 2011, that figure had increased sixteen-fold. What happened? The European Union expanded – twice – and with EU status comes the right to free movement between Member States. It didn't take long for many residents of the former Eastern Bloc to move west.

Now, more than three million of the 8.2 million Londoners hail from outside the UK. That's a million more than in 2001. Of these recent arrivals, nearly 40% came from the EU's twelve new member states (dark blue). The speed of these shifts is unprecedented. It took centuries for Ireland and India to reach 150,000 London residents. Poland did so in less than a decade. Meanwhile, the number of migrants from Ireland has decreased. Who knows what London will look like in 2021?

150,000   200,000   250,000 immigrants

Poland +136,000

India +89,500

Population in 2001

Country of birth of London residents, 2001-2011

— European Union members (pre-2001)   — Africa
— New EU members (2001-2011)   — Asia
— Europe (other)   — North America
                                              — Oceania
COUNTRIES WITH A POPULATION CHANGE   — South America & the Caribbean
OF LESS THAN 1,000 PEOPLE NOT SHOWN

Population growth rate for London, 2001-2011: **12%**

Ireland -27,700

150,000   200,000   250,000 immigrants

SOURCE: 2011 CENSUS, ONS

Passports, Please

Londoners are global citizens.

For the first time, the 2011 Census asked, 'What passports do you hold?' 5.8 million Londoners ticked 'United Kingdom'; 1.7 million named another country. In the map on this page, we show where London's 5.8 million British passport holders were born. Many came from India, Bangladesh, Pakistan, Jamaica and Kenya decades ago and have since gained British or dual citizenship.

Number of British passport holders in London by country of birth, 2011

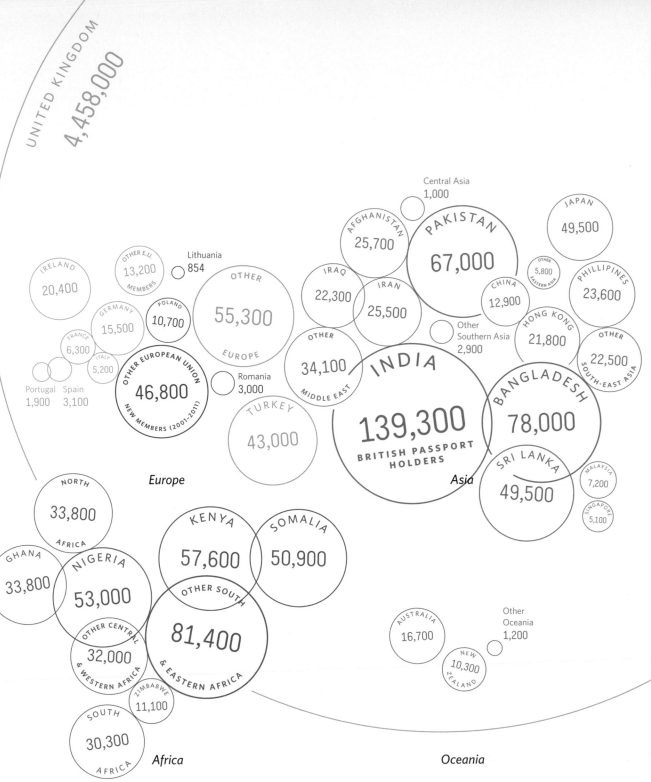

UNITED KINGDOM 4,458,000

Europe

IRELAND 20,400
OTHER E.U. 13,200 MEMBERS
Lithuania 854
GERMANY 15,500
FRANCE 6,300
POLAND 10,700
ITALY 5,200
Portugal 1,900
Spain 3,100
OTHER EUROPEAN UNION NEW MEMBERS (2001-2011) 46,800
OTHER 55,300 EUROPE
Romania 3,000
TURKEY 43,000

Asia

Central Asia 1,000
AFGHANISTAN 25,700
PAKISTAN 67,000
JAPAN 49,500
IRAQ 22,300
IRAN 25,500
CHINA 12,900
OTHER EASTERN ASIA 5,800
PHILLIPINES 23,600
OTHER 34,100 MIDDLE EAST
Other Southern Asia 2,900
HONG KONG 21,800
OTHER SOUTH-EAST ASIA 22,500
INDIA 139,300 BRITISH PASSPORT HOLDERS
BANGLADESH 78,000
SRI LANKA 49,500
MALAYSIA 7,200
SINGAPORE 5,100

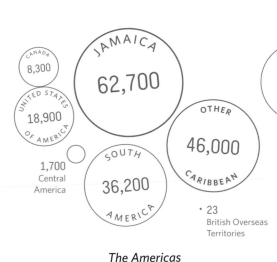

The Americas

CANADA 8,300
UNITED STATES OF AMERICA 18,900
1,700 Central America
JAMAICA 62,700
SOUTH AMERICA 36,200
OTHER CARIBBEAN 46,000
• 23 British Overseas Territories

Africa

NORTH AFRICA 33,800
GHANA 33,800
NIGERIA 53,000
OTHER CENTRAL & WESTERN AFRICA 32,000
ZIMBABWE 11,100
SOUTH AFRICA 30,300
KENYA 57,600
SOMALIA 50,900
OTHER SOUTH & EASTERN AFRICA 81,400

Oceania

AUSTRALIA 16,700
Other Oceania 1,200
NEW ZEALAND 10,300

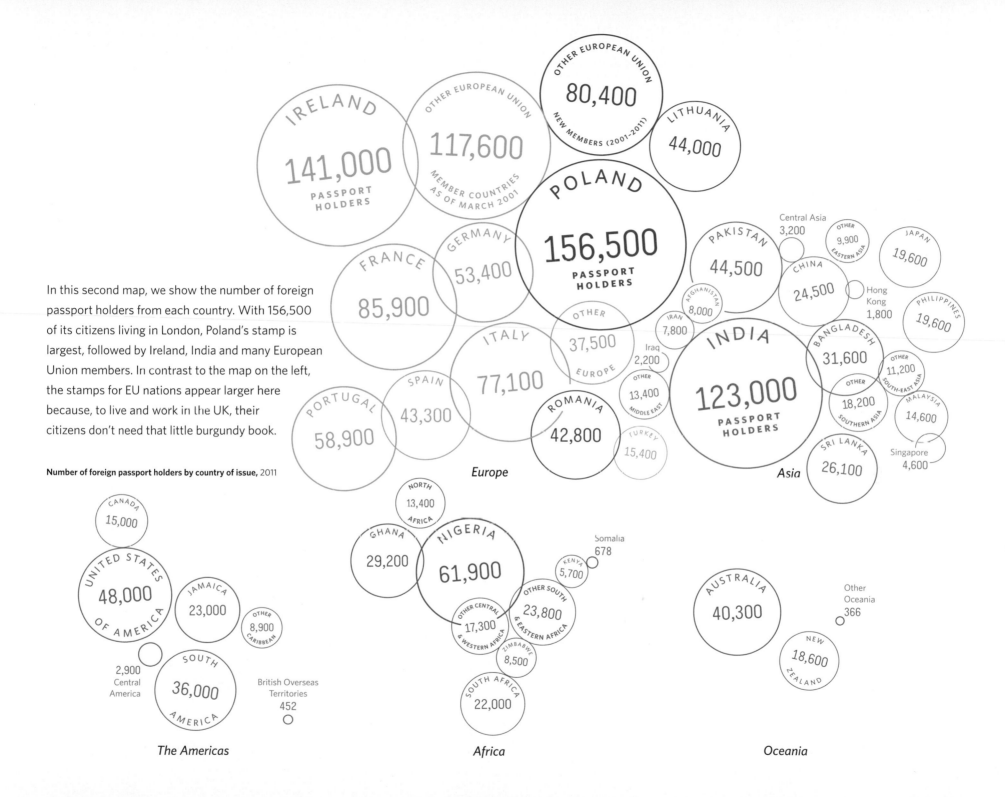

In this second map, we show the number of foreign passport holders from each country. With 156,500 of its citizens living in London, Poland's stamp is largest, followed by Ireland, India and many European Union members. In contrast to the map on the left, the stamps for EU nations appear larger here because, to live and work in the UK, their citizens don't need that little burgundy book.

Number of foreign passport holders by country of issue, 2011

IRELAND 141,000 PASSPORT HOLDERS

OTHER EUROPEAN UNION 117,600 MEMBER COUNTRIES AS OF MARCH 2001

OTHER EUROPEAN UNION 80,400 NEW MEMBERS (2001-2011)

LITHUANIA 44,000

POLAND 156,500 PASSPORT HOLDERS

FRANCE 85,900

GERMANY 53,400

PAKISTAN 44,500

Central Asia 3,200

OTHER EASTERN ASIA 9,900

JAPAN 19,600

CHINA 24,500

Hong Kong 1,800

PHILIPPINES 19,600

AFGHANISTAN 8,000

IRAN 7,800

OTHER 37,500 EUROPE

ITALY 77,100

Iraq 2,200

INDIA 123,000 PASSPORT HOLDERS

BANGLADESH 31,600

OTHER 11,200 SOUTH-EAST ASIA

OTHER 13,400 MIDDLE EAST

OTHER 18,200 SOUTHERN ASIA

MALAYSIA 14,600

PORTUGAL 58,900

SPAIN 43,300

ROMANIA 42,800

TURKEY 15,400

SRI LANKA 26,100

Singapore 4,600

Europe

Asia

CANADA 15,000

NORTH AFRICA 13,400

UNITED STATES 48,000 OF AMERICA

JAMAICA 23,000

OTHER 8,900 CARIBBEAN

GHANA 29,200

NIGERIA 61,900

Somalia 678

KENYA 5,700

AUSTRALIA 40,300

Other Oceania 366

2,900 Central America

SOUTH 36,000 AMERICA

British Overseas Territories 452

OTHER CENTRAL & WESTERN AFRICA 17,300

OTHER SOUTH & EASTERN AFRICA 23,800

ZIMBABWE 8,500

NEW ZEALAND 18,600

SOUTH AFRICA 22,000

The Americas

Africa

Oceania

Self-reported ethnicity
2011

Asian
- Indian
- Bangladeshi
- Pakistani
- Chinese
- Other

White
- English, Welsh, Scottish or N. Irish
- Irish
- Gypsy
- Other

Black
- African
- Caribbean
- Other

Mixed
- White + Asian
- White + African
- White + Caribbean

- Arab
- Other

ENFIELD
BARNET
HARROW
HARINGEY
WALTHAM FOREST
REDBRIDGE
HAVERING
BRENT
CAMDEN
ISLINGTON
HACKNEY
LEA VALLEY
NEWHAM
BARKING & DAGENHAM
EALING
WESTMINSTER
CITY
TOWER HAMLETS
HILLINGDON
KENSINGTON & CHELSEA
HAMMERSMITH & FULHAM
Hyde Park
River Thames
GREENWICH
HOUNSLOW
Heathrow Airport
SOUTHWARK
LAMBETH
LEWISHAM
BEXLEY
WANDSWORTH
RICHMOND UPON THAMES
Richmond Park
MERTON
KINGSTON UPON THAMES
SUTTON
CROYDON
BROMLEY

0   5 km

Asian

Bangladeshis cluster
in Tower Hamlets, the
first home for many
migrant communities.

Black

Many of the Jamaican
migrants who sailed in
on the *Empire Windrush*
in 1948 settled in Brixton.

Arab/Other

At the southern end of
Edgware Road you'll find
Lebanese restaurants
and Islamic banks.

White

Mixed

EthniCity

Few cities can match London's ethnic diversity.

This isn't a colour blindness test. But in a way it
could be. Fewer than 45% of Londoners consider
themselves 'White British'. Some see this statistic
as a symptom of unregulated immigration; others
see it as proof that London is and has always been
a global city. Whatever your views, there is no doubt
that generations of migrants – Irish, Jewish, Indian,
Jamaican and Polish, to name just a few – have helped
shape the city we know today.

Using data from the 2011 Census, we have counted
the number of people per self-reported ethnic group
across 25,270 small areas (each of which is home
to around 250 people). We then scattered coloured
dots within each of these areas for every twenty
people or so of the same ethnicity. Places with lots
of different coloured dots are therefore more diverse.
Patterns emerge where communities have developed
along with the amenities that serve them, such as
places of worship, specialist food shops and schools.
These in turn attract more people who value them.
In the smaller maps, we highlight some of these
communities. Those who identified themselves as
Asian tend to span from east to west, and as Black,
north to south. Unlike colour blindness, none of these
patterns are permanent. Londoners are often on the
move, so this map will never look the same again.

Counting the Invisible

In 2012, one researcher set out to document people the census couldn't see.

Over the course of a year, Shlomit Flint, a researcher at University College London, walked the streets of Whitechapel to better understand how the microdynamics of this one small, multicultural neighbourhood might influence the global city.

The 2011 Census counted about 9,000 individuals in this area. To her, that figure sounded low. So she went door-to-door from sunrise to well-past sunset, conducting a census of her own. In total, she visited 4,269 families in 47 community buildings and 1,615 privately owned flats. Having spent five years learning Arabic and Bengali to prepare for this survey, Flint gradually became part of the community. She met with local leaders, visited mosques and brought her children to the playground. In the end, she had tallied 13,000 individuals, 4,000 more than the official census. 'They think that they cover everything,' says Flint. 'I know that they only cover 70%.'

Just east of the City's wall, Whitechapel was transformed from a rural road to the bowels of Dickensian London and then to a 21st-century melting pot. With an influx of Eastern Europeans, it may be transforming yet again.

Self-reported ethnicity of families interviewed, 2012

- White British
- European Union members (pre-2001)
- E.U. accession countries (since 2001)
- Europe (other)
- Middle Eastern
- East Asian
- South Asian
- African
- Caribbean

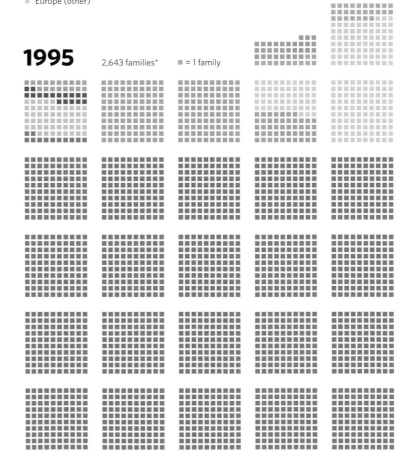

1995

2,643 families*   ■ = 1 family

2012

4,269 families

*There aren't more flats now then twenty years ago, so why are there so many more families? 'First, it's the overcrowding,' says Flint. 'In the area I examined, 40% are undocumented. In a flat that's supposed to have one family, they have actually 20 or 30 individuals.'

There were also fewer unknowns in 2012. To estimate how many families lived in the area in 1995, Flint asked the current tenants to remember from whom they bought their flat. But it wasn't always easy to determine who lived where in 1995.

WORD OF MOUTH

More than 80% of the tenants interviewed found their flats through word of mouth from family or a friend. South Asians and Africans were most likely to choose a place because of its neighbours rather than its price. 'It's very important for them to keep a separation of identity,' says Flint, 'and to live among their friends.'

Motives for choosing a flat by self-identified ethnicity, 2012

- Price
- Neighbours
- Institutions (e.g. churches, mosques, schools)

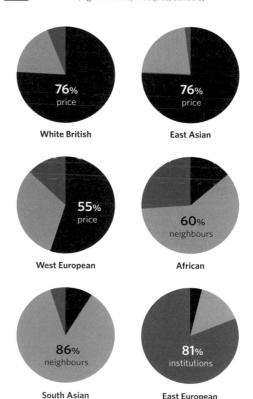

White British — 76% price

East Asian — 76% price

West European — 55% price

African — 60% neighbours

South Asian — 86% neighbours

East European — 81% institutions

Greetings From London

You say hello. I say cześć.

London boasts over 300 different spoken languages – more than any other city in the world. The capital's *lingua franca,* of course, remains English: 78% of Londoners cited it as their 'main' language in the 2011 Census. The other 22% speak in different tongues, including Urdu, Somali and Tagalog. We celebrate the city's linguistic diversity by mapping how you'd say 'hello' in the most frequently spoken languages aside from English. Each 'hello' has been scaled to show the percentage of people in each area who use it. Bengali is now the third most spoken language in the capital, behind Polish. So next time you are heading east of the City, give *salaam* a try, or *hola* south of the river. You might just get a *labas* or *olá* in return.

LANGUAGE FAMILIES

Romance

bonjour
French

ciao
Italian

olá
Portuguese

salut
Romanian

hola
Spanish

Germanic

guten tag
German

hej
Swedish

sholem aleykhem
Yiddish

Albanian

përshëndetje
Albanian

Balto-Slavic

labas
Lithuanian

cześć
Polish

privet
Russian

Hellenic

geia sou
Greek

Indo-Aryan

salaam
Bengali

kem cho
Gujarati

namaste
Hindi & Nepalese

sat sri akal
Punjabi

assalam-o-alekum
Urdu

Iranian

dorood
Persian/Farsi

Hindus who speak
Bengali say *nômoshkar;*
Muslims who speak
Punjabi say *salaam.*

Other

marhaban
Arabic

shalom
Hebrew

kamusta
Tagalog/Filipino

vanakkam
Tamil

merhaba
Turkish

ni hao
Chinese

konnichiwa
Japanese

anyoung haseyo
Korean

haye
Somali

kaabo
Yoruba

It is rare for a language to have only one way to say hello. We have done our best to match levels of formality and reflect the most popular usage. If in doubt, just say hi!

Percentage of people specifying this as their main language, 2011

hello | hello | hello | hello

5%   10   20

River Thames

WEMBLEY

A40

EALING

TRAINS TO PADDINGTON

Twitter Ink

London's online and offline worlds blend into one.

Each of the 9.4 million tweets splattered across this map tells us two things:
the location from where it was sent and the home town of the person who sent it.
Many of these 140-character messages were sent by visitors from countries such
as Turkey or Italy. We know this because Twitter users have the option of sharing
their location every time they post a message. If most of the messages in a user's
account were sent from Rome, we assumed this to be their 'home'.

Tweets from international tweeters fill the air in the city centre, where visitors
admire London's landmarks or do business in the City. Middle-eastern restaurants
along Edgware Road light up with tweets from Kuwaitis while passengers on
Turkish Airlines speckle Heathrow's Terminals 3 and 5. Grey tweets trace the path
of London's railways as British commuters take to Twitter to complain of delays
or to announce their arrival in the capital.

M4

A4

Terminals 1–3

Terminal 5

*Heathrow
Airport*

Terminal 4

Tweets by home country
September 2012 – November 2013

- ● Saudi Arabia
- ● Kuwait
- ● Turkey
- ● Spain
- ● France
- ● Italy
- ● United States
- ● UK
- ● Other

Each dot represents a single
tweet. Users who tweeted
multiple times created multiple
dots on the map. All are coloured
by their home countries.

CAMDEN

London
Zoo

Regent's Park

Euston
Station

HOXTON

OLD STREET

British
Museum

MARYLEBONE

Paddington
Station

SOHO

St Paul's
Cathedral

CITY OF LONDON

LIMEHOUSE

Marble
Arch

OXFORD STREET

MAYFAIR

NOTTING
HILL

Westfield
London

Hyde Park

Kensington
Gardens

Holland
Park

Green
Park

St James's
Park

STRAND

Tower
of London

Tate
Modern

London
Eye

London
Bridge
Station

EDGWARE ROAD

TRAINS TO PADDINGTON

HOLLOWAY ROAD

KINGSLAND ROAD

MILE END ROAD

TRAINS TO FENCHURCH STREET

Westfield
Stratford City

Victoria Park

Canary
Wharf

ISLE OF DOGS

River Thames

Buckingham
Palace

Houses of
Parliament

Elephant
and Castle

Earl's Court
Exhibition Building

SOUTH
KENSINGTON

Victoria
Station

KING'S ROAD

CHELSEA

TRAINS TO LONDON BRIDGE STATION

OLD KENT ROAD

GREENWICH

Greenwich
Park

Battersea
Park

TRAINS TO VICTORIA STATION

Clapham Junction
Station

BRIXTON

PUTNEY

0   3 km

SOURCES: ALISTAIR LEAK AND MUHAMMAD ADNAN, UNIVERSITY COLLEGE LONDON; TWITTER

1 0 7

Who London Inspired

From Mozart to Lenin, blue plaques commemorate those who called the city home.

Years before he took up painting, Vincent van Gogh came to London. He lived in Lambeth and worked at his uncle's gallery near the Strand. In a letter to his brother Theo, he said, 'I used to pass Westminster Bridge every morning and every evening and know how it looks when the sun sets behind Westminster Abbey and the Houses of Parliament.' Though he stayed only two years, the city left an impression. He returned at age 23 to teach Sunday school in Isleworth. One night after a long walk home, he wrote to Theo: 'I wished you could have seen those London streets when the twilight began to fall and the lamps were lit.'

To honour the influence the city has had on some of history's great minds, English Heritage and its predecessors have installed more than 900 blue clay roundels on buildings where they once lived or worked. As we show on the lifelines to the right, many like van Gogh went on to create defining works after walking 'those London streets'.

ARE YOU WORTHY?
The Blue Plaques Panel reviews about a hundred nominations a year. To be eligible, you must either be 100 years old or have been dead for twenty years. And:

- have resided in London
- be regarded as 'eminent' by a majority of your professional peers
- have made an important positive contribution to human welfare
  OR
- be so famous that a 'well-informed passer-by' recognizes your name

All of the above may not apply to **Vladimir Lenin** who lived here at 36 Tavistock Place in 1908, fourteen years before founding the Soviet Union.

100 Londoners commemorated with blue plaques

— Lifespan
— Period in London as noted on the plaque
● Age when the listed noteable works were created, discovered or achieved

Jimi Hendrix and **Handel** both lived at 23 Brook Street. Said Hendrix, 'I didn't even know this was Handel's pad. And, to tell you God's honest truth, I haven't heard much of the fella's stuff.'

The first blue plaque went up in 1867 at the birthplace of the poet **Lord Byron,** 24 Holles Street, where he lived until he was three. The house and plaque were torn down in 1889.

EDWARD
D. H. LAWRENCE
JAMES CLERK MAXWELL
ELIZABETH BROWNING
CHARLES DARWIN
SYLVIA PLATH
IAN FLEMING
ALEXANDER POPE
SIR ALFRED HITCHCOCK
SIMON BOLIVAR
AMY JOHNSON
RANDOLPH CALDECOTT
JIMI HENDRIX
VIRGINIA WOOLF
JOHN SNOW
CHARLES DICKENS
RUDYARD KIPLING
EZRA POUND
JOHN KEATS
ALDOUS HUXLEY
SAMUEL MORSE
VINCENT van GOGH
PERCY SHELLEY
MAHATMA GANDHI
BENJAMIN BRITTEN
MICHAEL FARADAY
SIR JOSEPH WILLIAM BAZALGETTE
SIR ERNEST SHACKLETON
WOLFGANG A. MOZART
JOHN RUSKIN
EVELYN WAUGH
ROBERT BADEN-POWELL
HENRY GRAY
W. B. YEATS
ALAN TURING
LORD BYRON

DADDY
CASINO ROYALE
THE RAPE OF THE LOCK
REAR WINDOW
GRAN COLOMBIA
SOLO FLIGHT RECORD, LONDON TO CAPE TOWN
THE HOUSE THAT JACK BUILT
ARE YOU EXPERIENCED?
MRS DALLOWAY
CHOLERA MAP
A TALE OF TWO CITIES
JUNGLE BOOK
IN A STATION OF THE METRO
TO AUTUMN
BRAVE NEW WORLD
MORSE CODE
STARRY NIGHT
ADONAIS
DANDI SALT MARCH
PETER GRIMES
ELECTROMAGNETIC FIELD
LONDON'S SEWERS
BRITISH ANTARCTIC EXPEDITION
THE MAGIC FLUTE
MODERN PAINTERS
VILE BODIES
SCOUTING FOR BOYS
GRAY'S ANATOMY
THE TOWER
TURING TEST
CHILDE HAROLD'S PILGRAMAGE

80 years old   70   60   50

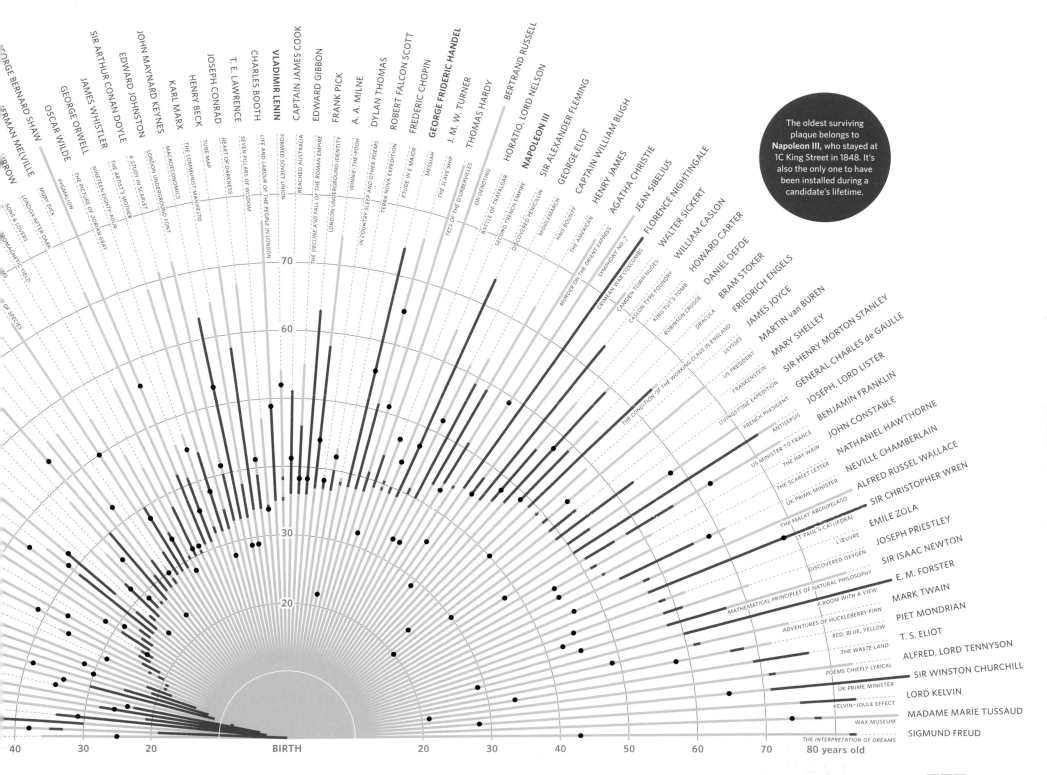

The oldest surviving plaque belongs to **Napoleon III,** who stayed at 1C King Street in 1848. It's also the only one to have been installed during a candidate's lifetime.

WHERE WE GO

Twitter Trips

Londoners go global.

Tweeting Londoners have become one
of the city's truly 21st-century exports.
Here we show where 120,000 of them
went between September 2012 and
November 2013. We defined London
tweeters as those who typically send
most of their messages from within the Greater London Authority
boundary. As they travelled abroad
for business or pleasure, they stayed
connected to share adventures in
140-character bursts. Each tweet
added to the arcs on this map. These
globetrotters made it to 3,600 places,
including Rome, Dubai, Las Vegas
and Disney World.

The tweets shown here are
but a sample of the millions
posted by Londoners. We
omitted spambots and users
who only sent a couple of
messages. Of the remainder,
not all had accurate location
information, so these were
also removed.

Number of Twitter users
September 2012 – November 2013

—— More than 1,000
—— 101–1,000
—— 11–100
—— 2–10

SOURCES: ALISTAIR LEAK AND MUHAMMAD ADNAN,
UNIVERSITY COLLEGE LONDON; TWITTER

NORTH AMERICA

Seattle

New York

Las Vegas

Dallas

Orlando

Honolulu

Mexico City

EQUATOR

PACIFIC

OCEAN

SOUTH AMERICA

Buenos Aires

Glasgow
Belfast
London
Berlin
EUROPE
Milan
Rome
Ibiza
Málaga

Canary
Islands

AFRICA

Lagos

Cape Town

ASIA

Jeddah

Dubai

Shanghai

Tokyo

Hong Kong

Singapore

ATLANTIC

OCEAN

INDIAN

OCEAN

AUSTRALIA

Melbourne

Sydney

Auckland

Not all lines go through
London because some
tweeters visited multiple
cities while travelling.

West Hampstead

Finsbury Park

Stratford

Camden
Town

Euston

Oxford
Circus

Moorgate
Liverpool St

Paddington

Fenchurch St

Charing Cross

London
Bridge

Canary
Wharf

Waterloo

Victoria

Elephant and Castle

Hammersmith

**Most exited rail stations
by origin location, 7–10 a.m.**
July – August 2012*

Nearly a million Londoners
sweep into work each morning
via Undergound, Overground
and National Rail. Here,
geographer Ed Manley
used Oyster card data to
show where most of
them exit the network.

*EXCLUDES THE OLYMPIC FORTNIGHT

Wimbledon

There is order and beauty in the chaos of your commute

Barking

Almost every journey taken in London leaves a digital trace in its wake. Flights are tracked, travel cards logged and minicabs monitored. It may be hard to appreciate as you squeeze onto a Tube or bus in the morning, but you are one of millions adding to the beauty of the currents captured in the following pages.

Take this graphic, for example. Geographer Ed Manley at University College London's Centre for Advanced Spatial Analysis used Oyster card data to trace 48.9 million morning commutes. He drew arcs between all of London's Underground, Overground and National Rail stations and their most popular destinations. Giving each destination a colour illustrates interdependencies between regions. For example, most traffic south of the Thames flows into only three stations: Waterloo, Victoria and London Bridge. Meanwhile, in the City's financial district, Liverpool Street and Fenchurch Street stations attract commuters from the eastern suburbs.

Looking at these city-wide flows, the transport system certainly appears

predictable. There's a fixed number of stations, a known number of trains and decent estimates of the likely number of passengers. Zoom into stations, however, and things become much more turbulent. People wrestle through barriers, down escalators, onto platforms and into trains. At this level, individual decisions count. If the same decision is made by thousands of people simultaneously – to bypass a delay on the Central line via the Piccadilly, for example – the entire network can feel the impact. While it may never be possible to predict the next signal failure or bus breakdown, we can explore the data from past service disruptions to anticipate how people will react in the future.

Think of all this commuter data like the River Thames. As it courses through the city, its flow is monitored at control centres around the capital. Transport for London (TfL) alone logs 24 million journeys a day across its network. Their controllers, planners and researchers aren't drowning; they're learning how to swim. For the first time, they can truly immerse themselves and develop ways to make our trains more reliable, our cyclists safer and, ultimately, our commutes faster.

TfL's biggest challenge, however, is keeping pace with demand. Technologies already exist to accommodate a million new commuters; you just need double-decker trains and longer station platforms. The problem is, these things can't be implemented without re-digging the entire Underground network. Crossrail may be the largest construction project in Europe (see pp. 56–7), but it will only increase rail transport capacity by 10%. With London's population growing 12% in ten years (see p. 78), the great hope is that data will allow 21st-century London to work better with what its steam-minded forebears laid down centuries ago.

FI 450
Reykjavik to
Heathrow

IRELAND

SHANNON

DL 618
Detroit to
Heathrow

Untangled On Arrival

The longest queues in London form overhead.

With 1,500 flights from more than 300 destinations arriving each day, aircraft contrails tie a giant bow over the city. Don't let this knotted appearance fool you. At Heathrow Airport, precise choreography guides a plane onto the tarmac every 150 seconds.

As they land, planes give off swirling 'wake turbulence'. Larger planes can handle flying through it, but smaller ones must wait for it to subside. In a perfect world, planes would arrive in order of size, smallest to largest. They don't, so air traffic controllers pace out incoming flights in circular holding patterns above London called 'stacks'. Four of the city's eight – Bovingdon, Lambourne, Ockham and Biggin Hill – service Heathrow exclusively. To see them up close, turn the page.

Arriving flights
22-23 August 2013

Europe
North America
Asia
Africa
South America & the Caribbean
Oceania

0   50 km

ATLANTIC

OCEAN

VS 64
Havana
to Gatwick

Celtic

Sea

SOURCE: FLIGHTRADAR24.COM

BNN
Bovingdon
Stack

FI 450
Reykjavik to
Heathrow

LAM
Lambourne
Stack

Luton
Airport

Stansted
Airport

BA 2
New York to
London City

BA 38
Beijing
to Heathrow

AI 111
Delhi to
Heathrow

GREATER LONDON
AUTHORITY
BOUNDARY

London City
Airport

River Thames

Heathrow
Airport

DL 618
Detroit to
Heathrow

BIG
Biggin Hill
Stack

OCK
Ockham
Stack

BA 248
Rio de Janeiro
to Heathrow

SA 234
Johannesburg
to Heathrow

EZY 2092
Ibiza to
Luton

VS 64
Havana to
Gatwick

Gatwick
Airport

JL 401
Tokyo to Heathrow ✈

*Southend
Airport*

Thames Estuary

┌─ ─ ─ ─ ─ ─ ─ ─ ─ ─ ─ ─ ─ ─ ─ ┐
│ *Proposed location for*   │
│ *'London Britannia Airport'* │
└─ ─ ─ ─ ─ ─ ─ ─ ─ ─ ─ ─ ─ ─ ─ ┘

Arriving flights
22–23 August 2013

Europe
North America
Asia
Africa
South America & the Caribbean
Oceania

0 ———————————— 10 km

To keep pace with global demand,
Heathrow hopes to build a third
runway. 'It's not about more
tarmac,' they argue. 'It's about
Britain's place in the world.' The
airport is competing with plans
for a bigger airport in the middle
of the Thames Estuary. Supporters say this would clear the skies
over London; critics fear an envi-
ronmental disaster. Either way,
London needs to decide soon if
it wants to remain a 'Hub for the
World' (see pp. 40-41).

LX 454
Zurich
to London City ✈

English Channel

Thames Gateway

The world converges on the city through its estuary.

Now that skyscrapers tower above the cranes on London's docks and wharves, many have forgotten that the Thames was once a gateway to the world. Perhaps for this reason, in January 2006, the sea gods sent Londoners a reminder of their city's nautical ties in the form of a northern bottlenose whale. Just as thousands of ships do each year, the maverick whale navigated the estuary's treacherous sand banks, past its relics of war and Southend's pleasure pier. It could have veered left up the River Medway and into Kent. Instead, it pressed on into the Yantlet Channel and the Thames proper, overtaking enormous container ships as they slowed to dock at Tilbury. Upstream, the Thames becomes too shallow for these 'supercarriers', so the whale was able to continue on alone. Turn the page to follow its journey.

The Port of London Authority covers 95 miles of the River Thames, overseeing the safe passage of thousands of vessels a year that contribute £3.7 billion to the UK economy. In this graphic we show only 24 hours of the action, which still features 334 tracks from ships registered in 26 different countries from Serbia to Hong Kong, Norway to Saint Vincent and the Grenadines.

Nautical traffic by vessel type, 12 April 2014

- Cargo
- Fishing
- Passenger/Pleasure
- Pilots & Tugs
- Other

- Anchorage
- Forts
- Wind farm
- Wrecks

- Tidal flats
- Shallows
- Deep water

0   5 km

SOURCES: FLEETMON.COM; OS

Nautical traffic by vessel type
12 April 2014

— Cargo
— Fishing
— Passenger/Pleasure
— Pilots & Tugs
— Other

0   1 km

Blackfriars Bridge
Millennium Bridge
Queenhithe Dock
Southwark Bridge
Cannon St Railway Bridge
London Bridge
Tate Modern
Bankside Pier
Golden Hinde II
HMS Belfast
Tower Bridge
Tower of London
St Katharine Docks
Upper Pool
Saint Saviour's Dock
Shadwell Basin
Lower Pool
Surrey Basin
Limehouse Reach
Greenland Dock
Limehouse Cut
River Lea
Bow Creek
West India Quay
East India Dock Basin
Blackwall Basin
South Dock
Millwall Inner Dock
ISLE OF DOGS
Millwall Outer Dock
Blackwall Reach
Emirates Air Line
Bugsby's Reach
Greenwich Reach
Deptford Creek
Cutty Sark
National Maritime Museum
Royal Observatory Greenwich
Royal Victoria Dock
Pontoon Dock
Royal Albert Dock
London City Airport
King George V Dock
North Woolwich Pier
Gallions Reach
Woolwich Reach
Thames Barrier
Woolwich Ferry
Woolwich Arsenal Pier
CREEKMOUTH
Barking Creek
Dagenham Docks
Ford Motor Works
Barking Reach
Halfway Reach
THAMESMEAD
Erith Marshes
Erith Reach
ERITH

The 'Thames Whale' was first sighted on 19 January 2006 by the Thames Barrier control team.

1

2

3

4

As the whale slipped past the Thames Barrier and towards the iconic meander, it swam through what John Burns famously described as 'liquid history'. Whales, or more precisely blubber, kick-started the development of London's first large-scale docks in this area in the 17th century. (Greenland Dock owes its name to the island's whaling seas.) Like the Docklands themselves, attitudes have changed. Thousands lined the river to will the 'Thames Whale' back to sea. Sadly, the whale did not survive, but its bones remain preserved in the Natural History Museum.

1 **CRIME AND PUNISHMENT**
In 1798 the 'Marine Police Force' was created to deter some 11,000 light-fingered Londoners on London's overcrowded docks. Nearby, the hangman's noose at the infamous 'Execution Dock' was rarely slack. Pirates from all over the world were sent to their deaths here by the British Admiralty. Once killed, they were hung in metal cages called 'gibbets' along the Thames as a warning against piracy.

RAINHAM

*Wennington
Marshes*

*Aveley
Marshes*

Mardyke

Erith Rands

*Dartford
Marshes*

River Darent

PURFLEET

Long Reach

Colbert Ferry
Terminal

Queen
Elizabeth II
Bridge

*Stone Ness
Lighthouse*

*Thames
Europort*

GREENHITHE

Fiddler's Reach

*Broadness
Lighthouse*

*Swanscombe
Marshes*

*Botany
Marshes*

GREATER LONDON
AUTHORITY
BOUNDARY

E S S E X

Northfleet Hope

Grain
Terminal

Northfleet Hope
Container Terminal

Tilbury Docks

TILBURY

London International
Cruise Terminal

Tilbury
Fort

*West Tilbury
Marshes*

Gravesend Reach

Tilbury to
Gravesend Ferry

GRAVESEND

Thames and Medway Canal

*Westcourt
Marshes*

K E N T

Mucking Creek

*London
Gateway*

*Mucking
Marshes*

Mucking Flats

EAST TILBURY

5

Lower Hope Reach

*East Tilbury
Marshes*

Coalhouse
Fort

• Cliffe Fort

*Higham
Marshes*

*Shorne
Marshes*

---

2 **GREENWICH**
Declared a UNESCO World Heritage site in 1997, London's 'green port' has gone from an invader's encampment to Tudor Palace and then Royal Naval College. Atop a hill in Greenwich Park, the world's east and west hemispheres meet at the Royal Observatory – the source of 'Greenwich Mean Time' and the 'Prime Meridian' – which has been the basis for global navigation systems since 1884.

3 **ISLE OF DOGS**
Enclosed by the Thames' distinctive meander, this oddly named place is at the heart of the Docklands' transition from boats to banks. Its etymology remains a mystery. Some say it's where Edward III kept his kennels; others cite a corruption of 'Isle of Ducks' or even 'Isle of Hogs' (the Bishop of London kept 5,000 of them there). It might just have been a miserable place to live.

4 **TATE AND LYLE**
Look closely at a tin of 'Lyle's Golden Syrup' and you will see 'Out of the strong came forth sweetness.' Britain's oldest brand should adapt its biblical motto to 'Out of the Thames came forth sweetness' since the river has been the primary means of importing its ingredients for more than 130 years. Even today, it owns a dock capable of handling 72,000 tons of raw sugar.

5 **HOPE REACH**
Just as the nomenclature of London's streets can reveal their origins and purpose, so too can the names along the river. This is perhaps most clear from 'Hope Reach', a stretch of the lower Thames where sailors lifted their anchors for the last time before heading out on voyages around the globe.

SOURCE: FLEETMON.COM; OS

MOST USED MODES OF TRANSPORT

**Most popular way to get
to work by home location,** 2011

- Car
- Tube, DLR
- Train
- Bus
- Walk
- Bike
- Other

ONLY UNDERGROUND, OVERGROUND, TRAM,
CROSSRAIL AND DOCKLANDS LIGHT RAILWAY
(DLR) LINES ARE SHOWN. NATIONAL RAIL
SERVICES ALSO CRISSCROSS THE CAPITAL.

Cars dominate the outskirts of
London, where many residents
drive to jobs in the suburbs.
Those fortunate enough to live
in Central London, start and end
their days with a leisurely walk.
When it opens in 2018, Crossrail
(see pp. 56–7) will create a purple
belt north of the Thames.

Getting to Work

Where we live colours how we choose to commute.

The Underground may be the best-known way to get around London, but it is not an option for everyone. Few stations exist south of the Thames, where sandy soil made it difficult to dig tunnels. In these areas, most residents say they take cars (blue), trains (purple) and buses (red) to work. Buses are the workhorses of London's transport system. In 2013 alone, riders took 2.4 billion journeys, almost double the number of Tube riders. Price may factor in. Regardless of distance, peak bus fare costs £1.45, half as much as a Tube journey through Central London and a fraction of one through all zones of the network (£5).

SECOND MOST USED

A clear divide emerges when you look at the second most used transport modes. To the north, the Tube is popular while those in the south board trains.

THIRD MOST USED

Buses and bikes speckle the map of London's third most popular transport modes. Some suburbanites leave their keys and Oyster card at home and walk.

SOURCE: 2011 CENSUS, ONS; OLIVER O'BRIEN, UNIVERSITY COLLEGE LONDON (TRANSPORT LINES)

To and Fro, on the Tube

For 150 years, the Underground has helped Londoners connect the dots.

In the 1850s, when Charles Pearson pitched the idea for the world's
first subterranean railway, even he was not so confident as to claim he
was developing a scheme capable of transporting every person in the world,
a sum then estimated at 1.2 billion. Today, this is precisely the number of journeys
taken on the Tube each year. Here we show a sample of 668,000 journeys
by Oyster card users during the first week of November 2009. Thick orange
lines represent the most travelled routes such as King's Cross St Pancras
to London Bridge or Canary Wharf to North Greenwich.

SOURCE: TRANSPORT FOR LONDON

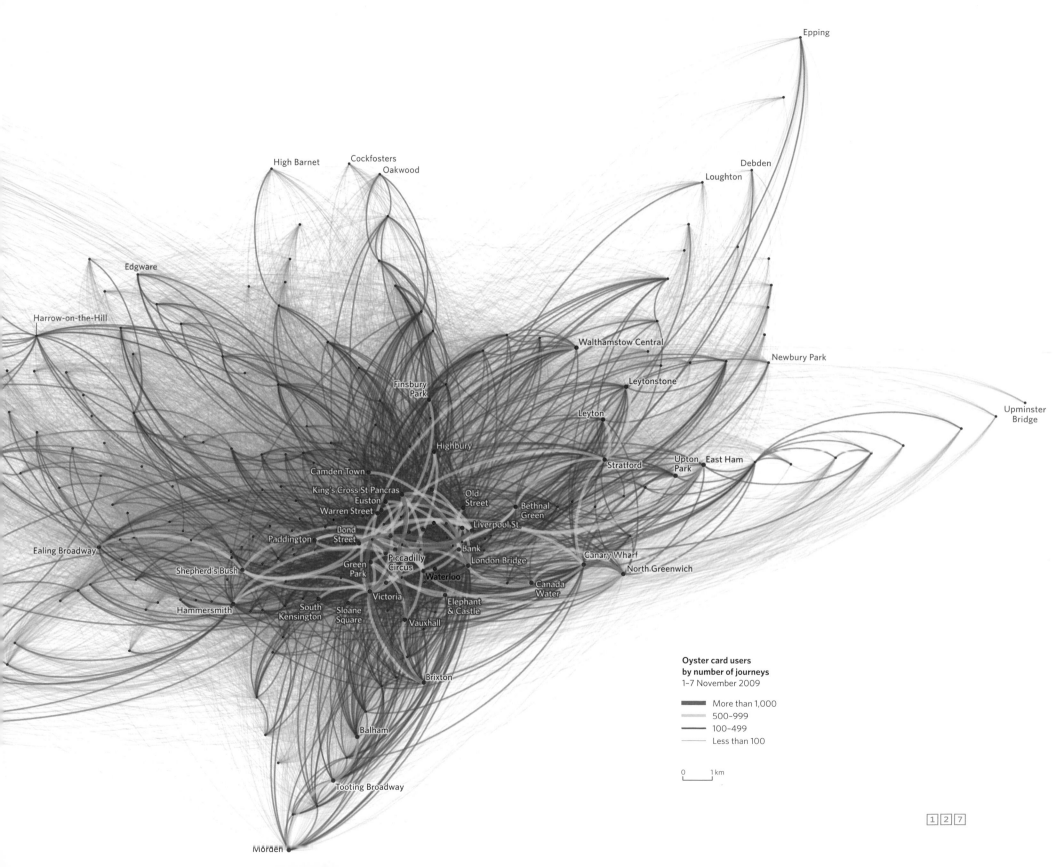

Epping

High Barnet   Cockfosters
                     Oakwood   Debden
                                                            Loughton

Edgware

Harrow-on-the-Hill   Walthamstow Central
                                                                                                    Newbury Park

                                                                        Leytonstone

                                 Finsbury
                                  Park   Leyton   Upminster
                                                                                                         Bridge

                                              Highbury

Ealing Broadway   Camden Town   Stratford   Upton   East Ham
                                                                                          Park
                          King's Cross St Pancras
                             Euston   Old
                          Warren Street   Street   Bethnal
                                                            Green
                                              Liverpool St.
                          Paddington   Bond   Canary Wharf
                                          Street   Bank
Shepherd's Bush   London Bridge   North Greenwich
                                    Green   Piccadilly
                                    Park   Circus
                                          Waterloo
                          Victoria   Canada
Hammersmith   South   Water
                 Kensington   Sloane   Elephant
                               Square   & Castle
                                      Vauxhall

                                                                    Oyster card users
                                                                    by number of journeys
                                      Brixton   1–7 November 2009

                                                                    ━━━ More than 1,000
                                                                    ─── 500–999
                                                                    ─── 100–499
                        Balham   ─── Less than 100

                                                                    ├────┤
                                                                    0   1 km
              Tooting Broadway

Morden   1 2 7

A Week on the Underground

Record-breaking traffic puts the Tube's health to the test.

During the first full week of the 2012 Olympic Games, London Underground broke its all-time ridership record – three times. 4.25 million passengers boarded on Tuesday, followed by 4.3 on Wednesday and 4.4 on Friday. To check the network's vitals, Jon Reades, a geographer at King's College London, administered an electrocardiogram of sorts. The waveforms

below represent the number of Oyster card users entering and exiting 258 stations from Sunday 29 July to Saturday 4 August. Stations are grouped and coloured by the lines they serve. His diagnosis? Activity peaked during the morning and evening commutes. Nothing too irregular there other than the volume of people pumping through the system.

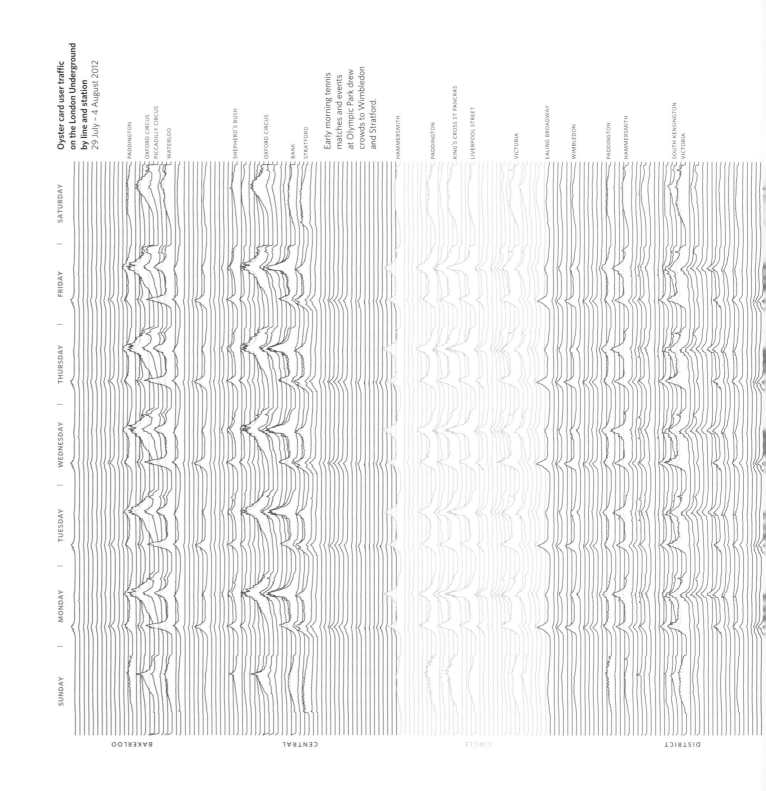

Oyster card user traffic on the London Underground by line and station
29 July – 4 August 2012

Early morning tennis matches and events at Olympic Park drew crowds to Wimbledon and Stratford.

SUNDAY   MONDAY   TUESDAY   WEDNESDAY   THURSDAY   FRIDAY   SATURDAY

PADDINGTON
OXFORD CIRCUS
PICCADILLY CIRCUS
WATERLOO

SHEPHERD'S BUSH
OXFORD CIRCUS
BANK
STRATFORD

HAMMERSMITH

PADDINGTON
KING'S CROSS ST PANCRAS
LIVERPOOL STREET

VICTORIA

EALING BROADWAY

WIMBLEDON

PADDINGTON
HAMMERSMITH

SOUTH KENSINGTON
VICTORIA

BAKERLOO

CENTRAL

CIRCLE

DISTRICT

HAMMERSMITH
PADDINGTON
BAKER STREET
KING'S CROSS ST PANCRAS
LIVERPOOL STREET

The Games brought heavy flows into London via railway stations like King's Cross St Pancras, Waterloo and Paddington.

BOND STREET
WATERLOO
LONDON BRIDGE
CANARY WHARF
STRATFORD

Stations near financial centres like Canary Wharf, Bank and Liverpool Street saw their heartbeats spike on weekdays. By Saturday they slowed to a murmur.

BAKER STREET
KING'S CROSS ST PANCRAS
LIVERPOOL STREET

WATERLOO
LONDON BRIDGE
BANK
LEICESTER SQUARE
ANGEL
KING'S CROSS ST PANCRAS
CAMDEN TOWN

Areas with nightlife such as Piccadilly and Leicester Square experienced a third peak before midnight, especially at the weekend.

HAMMERSMITH
SOUTH KENSINGTON
PICCADILLY CIRCUS
LEICESTER SQUARE
HOLBORN
KING'S CROSS ST PANCRAS

KING'S CROSS ST PANCRAS
OXFORD CIRCUS
VICTORIA

WATERLOO

SOURCE: TRANSPORT FOR LONDON

SUNDAY | MONDAY | TUESDAY | WEDNESDAY | THURSDAY | FRIDAY | SATURDAY

HAMMERSMITH & CITY

JUBILEE

METROPOLITAN

NORTHERN

PICCADILLY

VICTORIA

WATERLOO & CITY

WHERE WE GO

Around the World in 10 Lines

Every day, the Tube covers enough track to circle the globe five times.

Think you have a long Tube ride? In total, the trains of the London Underground network log more than 75 million kilometres a year. That's like circling the Earth at the Equator 1,900 times – or five times a day. Assuming such a journey were possible, if you boarded a carriage due south of London where the Prime Meridian meets the Equator and headed east, the Piccadilly Line – which led all lines with nearly 33,000 kilometres per day – would take you 80% of the way round as it passed through Gabon, Somalia, Indonesia and traversed the Indian and Pacific Oceans. It wouldn't be until deep in the Amazon that you'd transfer to the Central Line to make your way back to the Prime Meridian and begin your second loop.

Average kilometres operated per day by London Underground line
April 2012 – March 2013

0°
Prime Meridian

9° 21'E
Coast of Gabon

29° 17'E
Butembo, Democratic Republic of the Congo

33° 0'E
Lake Victoria

42° 30'E
Coast of Somalia

48° 30'W
Mouth of the Amazon

78° 49'W
Quito, Ecuador

91° 13'W
Galapagos Islands

ATLANTIC OCEAN

PICCADILLY LINE 32,731 km operated

CENTRAL 32,436 km

NORTHERN 31,648 km

DISTRICT 26,123 km

METROPOLITAN 19,665 km

BAKERLOO 9,679 km

CENTRAL

DISTRICT

METROPOLITAN

NORTHERN

CIRCLE / HAMMERSMITH & CITY 10,865 km

METROPOLITAN

JUBILEE

CENTRAL

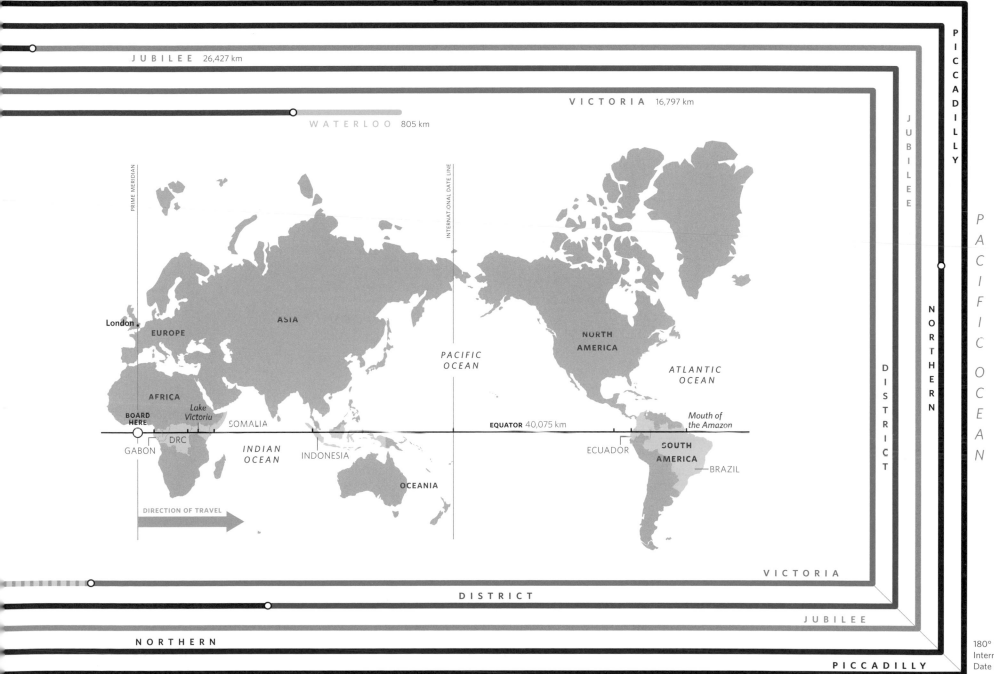

INDIAN OCEAN

98° 12'E
Coast of Indonesia

JUBILEE 26,427 km

WATERLOO 805 km

VICTORIA 16,797 km

PICCADILLY

JUBILEE

NORTHERN

DISTRICT

PACIFIC OCEAN

PRIME MERIDIAN

INTERNATIONAL DATE LINE

London

EUROPE

ASIA

NORTH
AMERICA

PACIFIC
OCEAN

ATLANTIC
OCEAN

AFRICA

Lake
Victoria

BOARD
HERE

SOMALIA

EQUATOR 40,075 km

Mouth of
the Amazon

GABON

DRC

INDONESIA

INDIAN
OCEAN

ECUADOR

SOUTH
AMERICA

BRAZIL

OCEANIA

DIRECTION OF TRAVEL

VICTORIA

DISTRICT

JUBILEE

NORTHERN

180°
International
Date Line

PICCADILLY

PACIFIC OCEAN

SOURCE: TRANSPORT FOR LONDON

1 3 1

Disrupted

As the Tube improves, Londoners may only have the weather left to complain about.

To commuters, every second counts. Any time shaved off a journey will accumulate to minutes and even hours over the course of a year. The opposite is also true. Delays on the Tube cost passengers 1.86 billion hours in the year ending March 2014. That's actually good news. The figure is less than half of what it was ten years ago. And that's not all. Over the past decade, there have been 600 fewer station closures, 4,600 fewer delays caused by staff or signal failures (see chart) and 2,000 fewer delays lasting longer than fifteen minutes – all of which has dropped the average wait time to one minute from a little over two. Preparations for the Olympics certainly sparked improvement. Since 2011, more than 97% of the scheduled trains have shown up on time. Better still, when things do go bad now, response times are quicker.

12,162 incidents
Average delay
6 minutes

12,000 INCIDENTS

STAFF DELAYS

9,000

Staff-related delays are down 29% since 2003. This is amazing considering current demand. Victoria Line drivers have just 218 seconds to change over when they reach the end of the line.

8,642 incidents
Average delay
5.5 minutes

6,000 INCIDENTS

3,631 incidents
Average delay
16 minutes

3,000 INCIDENTS

SIGNAL FAILURES

Suicides are the only cause of delay that has gone up – but not by much. There have been an average of 40 suicides per year since 2003.

2,498 incidents
Average delay
13 minutes

39 incidents
Average delay
76 minutes

SUICIDES

50 incidents
Average delay
68 minutes

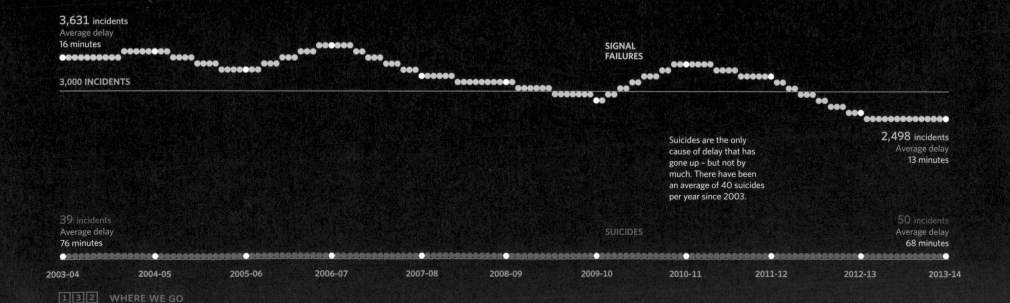

2003-04   2004-05   2005-06   2006-07   2007-08   2008-09   2009-10   2010-11   2011-12   2012-13   2013-14

TOTAL INCIDENTS	2003	04	05	06	07	08	09	10	11	12	2013		UNDERGROUND LINE
147												55:92	Northern
116												27:89	Central
107												34:73	Piccadilly
93												62:31	District
81												27:54	Victoria
60												31:29	Metropolitan
44												25:19	H&C
39												12:27	Jubilee
38												14:24	Bakerloo
TOTAL NONFATAL ATTEMPTS	11	10	10	9	21	28	40	39	46	37	36		
TOTAL SUICIDES	35	34	36	41	42	39	42	41	37	46	45		

Fortunately, Tube riders aren't greeted with this LED display when they enter a station. It compares nonfatal suicide attempts per line (yellow) to the number of fatal ones (orange). Over the past ten years, most incidents have occurred on the heavily travelled Northern, Central and Piccadilly lines.

SOURCE: TRANSPORT FOR LONDON

The Tube Challenge

Here's how to visit all 270 tube stations in one day.

If, while waiting for a train at Chesham station one morning, you glance over to see a few super-excited joggers holding a stopwatch, video camera and a dozen energy bars, think nothing of it – unless you happen to see them again sixteen hours later exiting a train at Heathrow's Terminal 5. In that case, offer to sign their logbook. You could be a witness to history.

The *Guinness Book of Records* credits R. J. Lewis and D. R. Longley with completing the first Tube Challenge on 13 June 1959. Since then, the game has evolved with the Tube map. Yet the essential rule remains: visit every station. To do so requires meticulous planning; endurance helps too for running between stations. Given the effort involved, Tube Challengers are understandably secretive about their routes. Andi James and Steve Wilson only released their record-setting route from 2009 (adapted here) after setting a new record – 16 hours, 29 minutes and 13 seconds – on 27 May 2011. The mark stood for two years. Then Geoff Marshall and Anthony Smith beat it by eight minutes and forty-six seconds on 16 August 2013.

THE BASICS

1 You don't have to cover every stretch of track or step on every platform, but you must arrive at or depart from every Underground station by train. (Overground, National Rail and Docklands Light Railway stations not included).

2 You may take buses or run between stations.

3 You must keep a log.

4 An independent witness must start and stop a master stopwatch at the beginning and end of the attempt.

For a full list of rules, go to *www.tubeforum.co.uk/rules*

To commemorate the Tube's 150th anniversary in 2013, Art on the Underground invited artist Mark Wallinger to create 270 original works, one for each station. He made labyrinths. Each one is unique and numbered in order of the stations visited on the route to the right.

START ✕ Chesham
6:20:00 a.m.

Watford

West Ruislip

Ickenham   0.7

North Harrow

Rayners Lane   0.7 miles

Uxbridge

East Acton

Ealing Broadway

Ealing Common

Richmond

FINISH
Heathrow Terminal 5
11:04:16 p.m.

SOURCE: ART ON THE UNDERGROUND, TRANSPORT FOR LONDON. PHOTO: OLIVER UBERTI

Harrow &
Wealdstone

Kenton

0.3

Northwick
Park

Preston
Road

Canons
Park

1.0

Edgware

Mill Hill
East

High Barnet

2.3

Cockfosters

Epping

Snaresbrook

2.2

Walthamstow
Central

Upminster

Baker
Street

Edgware
Road

Shepherd's
Bush

White
City

0.9

Olympia

Goodge
Street

Moorgate

Aldgate

0.2

Aldgate
East

West
Kensington

Sloane
Square

London
Bridge

Southwark

River Thames

Wimbledon

Kennington

Brixton

1.6

Morden

1 3 5

Route Masters

The next bus is closer than you think.

Londoners often say, 'I waited ages for a bus and then they all turned up at once.' If all the scheduled buses actually did arrive at the same time, you would be stuck in a long, red traffic jam. Transport researcher Joan Serras used these schedules to determine how many buses pass each of London's 22,565 bus stops each day. He then mapped the routes buses would take between them. Roads with more buses running along them appear wider and redder; those with fewer buses are narrower and paler. Roads with no buses have been excluded. In total, his map shows 114,000 daily trips. Next time you can't find a bus, try Waterloo Bridge. There, one crosses the Thames every sixteen seconds.

AREA ENLARGED

Number of daily bus trips in thousands, 2012

- More than 8
- 6–8
- 4–6
- Less than 4

0   5 km

SOURCE: NATIONAL PUBLIC TRANSPORT DATA REPOSITORY

Brent Cross
Shopping Centre

BARNET

BRENT

EDGWARE ROAD

EALING

WESTMINSTER

HOUNSLOW

Shepherd's Bush
Station

KENSINGTON
& CHELSEA

Hammersmith
Station

HAMMERSMITH
& FULHAM

Putney
Bridge

0   1 km

WANDSWORTH

HARINGEY

WALTHAM
FOREST

REDBRIDGE

Redbridge
Station

Stoke
Newington
Station

HACKNEY

Ilford
Station

ISLINGTON

CAMDEN

Queen Elizabeth
Olympic Park

Stratford
Station

NEWHAM

Regent's
Park

King's Cross
St Pancras
Station

KINGSLAND ROAD

PENTONVILLE RD

CITY ROAD

Euston
Station

TOWER HAMLETS

MARYLEBONE ROAD

British
Museum

BISHOPSGATE

Marble
Arch

OXFORD ST

REGENT ST

KINGSWAY

CITY

St Paul's
Cathedral

Monument

Tower
of London

London City
Airport

Trafalgar
Square

STRAND

Waterloo
Bridge

London
Bridge

Canary
Wharf

Blackwall
Tunnel

Hyde Park

PARK LANE

Buckingham
Palace

Westminster
Bridge

Elephant
and Castle
Station

River Thames

Westminster
Abbey

SOUTHWARK

Victoria
Station

Vauxhall
Bridge

Battersea
Park

OLD KENT ROAD

GREENWICH

LAMBETH

LEWISHAM

Lewisham
Station

Mental Maps

To become a London cabbie, memorize the map on the left.

They call it 'The Knowledge' – 320 taxi routes within a six-mile radius that extends from Charing Cross east to the Lea Valley, west to Chiswick, up to Alexandra Palace and down to Crystal Palace. Learn these 'runs' and you're barely halfway there. Then you just need to know the names and locations of all the streets, businesses and landmarks within a quarter-mile radius of each end (yellow circles).

'We call it the Dumbbell Effect,' says Malcolm Linskey, managing director of Knowledge Point School in Islington. Examiners never ask trainees to recite the exact runs in his books, such as No. 1: Manor House Station to Gibson Square (right). Instead, 'they'll say take me from John Scott Health Centre to the Almeida Theatre,' says Linskey, 'which is effectively the same route, but they got to know how to link up onto the route and how to come off at the other end.'

With 60,000 streets and more than 100,000 'points of interest' within those yellow circles, it takes most trainees two to four years to acquire The Knowledge. So why do it? With that Black Cab and green badge come certain perks: good pay, flexible hours, local pride, even a larger hippocampus (the area of the brain that governs spatial awareness and memory). As Linskey says, 'Once a cabbie's done it, he don't need a map anymore.'

Unlike minicab drivers who often rely on satellite navigation, London cabbies drive by memory. Frequently, they use side streets to get from A to B on the straightest line possible. To see how more Knowledge routes compare with Google Maps, turn the page.

ROUTE NO. 1
Manor House Station to Gibson Square

Leave on the left of Green Lanes
Right on Brownswood Road
Left on Blackstock Road
Forward on Highbury Park
Forward on Highbury Grove
Right on St Paul's Road
Comply Highbury Corner
Leave by Upper Street
Right on Islington Park Street
Left on College Cross
Right on Barnsbury Street
Left on Milner Square
Forward on Milner Place
Facing Gibson Square

Featured run

0   1 km

Regent's Park

EUSTON RD

SOUTHAMPTON ROW

GEORGE ST

OXFORD ST

Paddington Station

Australian High Commission

Hyde Park

British Museum

Green Park

St James's Park

THE MALL

BUCKINGHAM PALACE RD

Buckingham Palace

WESTMINSTER BRIDGE

Green Park

St James's Park

VAUXHALL BRIDGE

The Knowledge
Google Maps
Straight line

0   1 km

REGENCY ST

VAUXHALL BRIDGE

KENNINGTON RD

The Oval

BRIXTON RD

River Thames

CHELSEA BRIDGE

River Thames

Battersea Park

QUEENSTOWN RD

WANDSWORTH RD

Loughborough Junction Station

Elspeth Road

Clapham Common

ROUTE NO. 5
**Australian High Commission
to Paddington Station**

Leave on the right of Strand
Right on Aldwych
Left on Catherine Street
Right on Russell Street
Left on Drury Lane
Left on High Holborn
Forward on Princes Circus
Forward on St Giles High Street
Right on Earnshaw Street
Left on New Oxford Street
Forward on St Giles Circus
Forward on Oxford Street
Right on Great Portland Street
Left on Margaret Street
Comply Cavendish Square
Leave by Henrietta Place
Right on Wimpole Street
Left on Wigmore Street
Right on Duke Street
Comply Manchester Square
Leave by Manchester Street
Left on George Street
Right on Edgware Road
Left on Harrow Road
Comply Bishop's Bridge Roundabout
Leave by Bishop's Bridge Road
Left on Paddington Taxi Road

ROUTE NO. 93
**Buckingham Palace
to Loughborough Junction Station**

Comply Queen Victoria Memorial
Leave by Spur Road
Right on Birdcage Walk
Left on Buckingham Gate
Forward on Artillery Row
Left on Greycoat Place
Right on Horseferry Road
Right on Regency Place
Forward on Regency Street
Left on Vauxhall Bridge Road
Forward on Bessborough Gardens, Vauxhall Bridge, Bridgefoot, Vauxhall Cross, Kennington Lane
Right on Durham Street
Left on Harleyford Road
Forward on Kennington Oval, Harleyford Street, Camberwell New Road
Right on Brixton Road
Left on Loughborough Road
Left on Coldharbour Lane

ROUTE NO. 84
**British Museum
to Elspeth Road**

Leave on the right of Great Russell St
Left on Bloomsbury Street
Forward on Shaftesbury Avenue
Right on Princes Circus
Left on Shaftesbury Avenue
Left on Monmouth Street
Comply Seven Dials
Leave by Monmouth Street
Forward on Upper St Martins Lane

Right on Cranbourn Street
Left on Charing Cross Road
Forward on St Martin's Place, Trafalgar Square
Comply King Charles Island
Leave by Admiralty Arch
Forward on The Mall
Comply Queen Victoria Memorial
Leave by Spur Road

Right on Birdcage Walk
Forward on Buckingham Gate, Buckingham Palace Rd, Ebury Bridge Rd
Left on Chelsea Bridge Road
Forward on Chelsea Bridge, Queenstown Road
Comply Queen's Circus
Leave by Queenstown Road
Right on Lavender Hill

Euston Station

Lincoln's Inn Fields

SOUTHAMPTON ROW

GOWER ST

Hyde Park

SHAFTESBURY AVE

PICCADILLY

STRAND

THE MALL

St James's Park

WATERLOO BRIDGE

BROMPTON RD

St James's Park

FULHAM RD

KING'S RD

LAMBETH BRIDGE

KENNINGTON RD

Chelsea & Westminster Hospital

Albert Bridge

River Thames

Battersea Park

BRIXTON RD

LATCHMERE RD

Clapham Common

SOUTH LAMBETH RD

SOUTH CIRCULAR

ROUTE NO. 121
Euston Station to Brixton Prison

Leave on the left of Melton Street
Right on Euston Road
Left on Gower Street
Forward on Bedford Square,
Bloomsbury Street, Shaftesbury Avenue
Right on Princes Circus
Left on Shaftesbury Avenue
Left on Monmouth Street
Comply Seven Dials
Leave by Monmouth Street
Forward on Upper St Martin's Lane
Right on Cranbourn Street
Left on Charing Cross Road
Forward on St Martin's Place, Trafalgar Square,
Whitehall, Parliament Street, Parliament Square,
St Margaret Street, Old Palace Yard,
Abingdon Street, Millbank
Comply Millbank Circus
Leave by Lambeth Bridge
Comply Lambeth Circus
Leave by Albert Embankment
Left on Kennington Lane
Right on South Lambeth Road
Left on Stockwell Terrace
Righ on Clapham Road
Left on Stockwell Road
Left on Stockwell Park Walk
Right on Brixton Road
Forward on Brixton Hill
Right on Jebb Avenue

BRIXTON HILL

Brixton Prison

ROUTE NO. 124
Albert Bridge to Streatham Common

Leave by Albert Bridge Road
Bear right on Cambridge Road
Left on Battersea Bridge Road
Forward on Latchmere Road
Forward on Elspeth Road
Left on Clapham Common Northside
Right on The Avenue
Right on Clapham Common Southside
Forward on Balham Hill
Forward on Balham High Road
Left on Bedford Hill
Right on Garrad's Road
Left on Tooting Bec Gardens
Right on Streatham High Road
Left on Streatham Common North

ROUTE NO. 317
Chelsea & Westminster Hospital to Lincoln's Inn Fields

Leave on the right of Fulham Road
Right on Dovehouse Street
Left on Britten Street
Right on Astell Street
Left on Burnsall Street
Left on King's Road
Comply Sloane Square
Leave by Cliveden Place
Forward Eaton Gate, Eaton Square,
Hobart Place, Lower Grosvenor Place
Left on Buckingham Palace Road
Forward on Buckingham Gate
Forward on Queen Victoria Memorial
Right on The Mall
Forward on Admiralty Arch
Comply King Charles Island
Leave by Trafalgar Square
Right on Duncannon Street
Left on Strand
Left on Aldwych
Left on Kingsway
Right on Remnant Street

BEDFORD HILL

STREATHAM HIGH RD

Tooting Bec Common

Streatham Common

SOURCES: TAXI TRADE PROMOTIONS, GOOGLE

Minicab Corridors

The paths of minicab drivers redraw the map of London's motorways.

With their knowledge of side streets and shortcuts, London's iconic black cabs have the run of the city. Their unmetered rivals, the city's 67,000 minicabs, travel further afield on pre-arranged prices, often ushering passengers to destinations outside The Knowledge's six-mile radius (see pp. 138–141). With dispatchers tracking their efficiency via GPS, minicab drivers tend to stick to the routes recommended by their trusty SatNavs.

Using three months' worth of these GPS points, Ed Manley at University College London's Centre for Advanced Spatial Analysis wove the web of driver behaviour you see here. Every time a minicab passed between two junctions on the road network, he drew a line. More lines meant stronger connections. The stronger the connection, the more likely a driver was to use those roads together.

To distinguish these regional clusters, Manley added colour. For example, the reds of the M4 signal journeys to and from Heathrow Airport, while the many hues of the M25 and North Circular suggest, as Manley puts it, 'Drivers don't get on and travel around. They travel for a bit and then get off again.'

Minicab journeys
December 2010 – February 2011

Whilst major arteries can be discerned, this map does not trace roads. It depicts straight lines between junctions passed through by the minicabs. On the outskirts, coloured clusters appear larger and sparser because there are fewer junctions.

SOURCE: ADDISON LEE

To St Albans

LONDON ORBITAL

To Hertford

M25

To Stansted Airport

A10

M1

M11

To Chelmsford

NORTH CIRCULAR

A12

To Oxford

M25

A40

CAMDEN

STRATFORD

A13

PADDINGTON

SHOREDITCH

SOHO

River Thames

Hyde Park

THE CITY

CANARY WHARF

M4

CHELSEA

Heathrow Airport

FULHAM

GREENWICH

To Southend-on-Sea

A282

Queen Elizabeth II Bridge

A2

SOUTH CIRCULAR

To Canterbury

M25

A20

To Maidstone

A3

To Southampton

A23

LONDON ORBITAL

M25

To Sevenoaks

0   10 km

To Gatwick Airport

1 4 3

Lost & Found

Heathrow logs all that we leave behind.

Visitors to London leave more than digital traces on the city. They leave physical traces too – tens of thousands of them. In 2013 alone, the lost property office at Heathrow Airport logged 34,000 items (shown to the right), including violins, rings, stuffed animals, cars, a kayak, a Rottweiler and a phonograph.

Think that's a lot? Transport for London's Lost Property Office stockpiles more than 240,000 items a year found on the city's trains, buses and black cabs. Like Heathrow, they hold everything for three months. During the high travel season from July to September 2013, roughly one in five items were reclaimed at a rate of about 160 per day. While most retrievals occur at their office on Baker Street, TfL posts 50 or so items a month overseas.

In the chaos of travel, arriving home without a phone, sunglasses or jewellery appears to be a common enough mistake. Although you have to wonder how 100 travellers got far without their walking sticks.

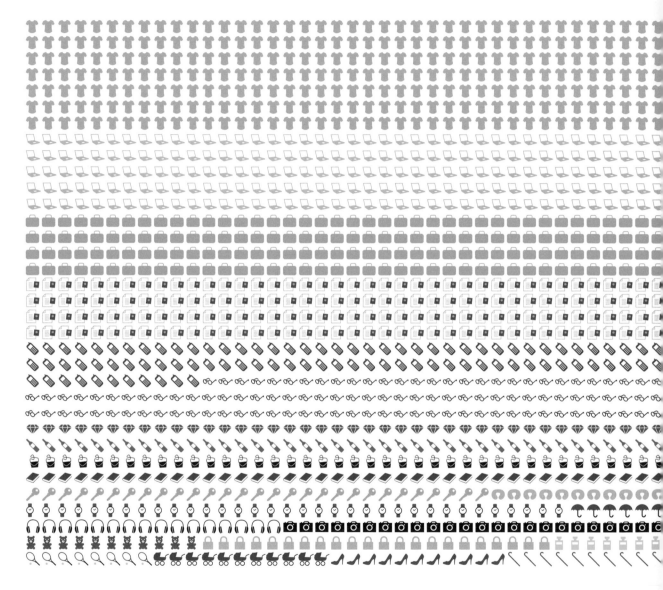

Items lost at Heathrow Airport, 2013   EACH ICON = 10 ITEMS

Clothes 6,570

Computers, tablets and electronics 5,090

Luggage 4,160

Passports, IDs and security documents 3,710

Mobile phones 2,580

Glasses and sunglasses 2,380

Jewellery 1,250

Duty-free items and food 1,110

Purses and wallets 1,060

Books and magazines 730

Keys 650

Neck pillows, blankets and mats 540

Watches 510

Umbrellas 430

Headphones 390

Photo and video equipment 390

Art 330

Toys and games 230

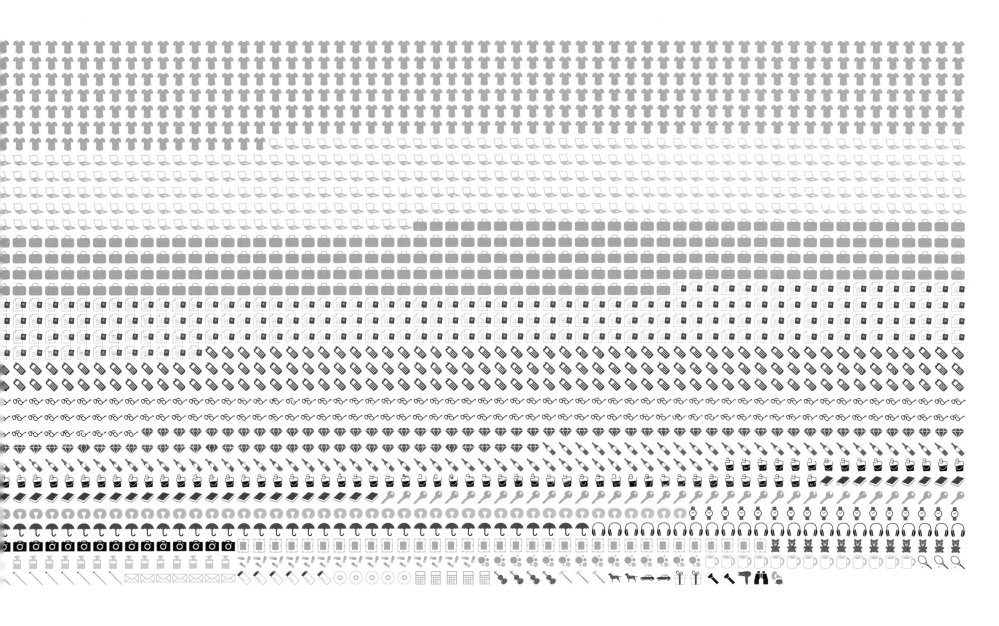

🔒 Safes and money storage 220	🛒 Baby supplies 110	◉ CDs and DVDs 50	🎁 Gifts 20
Perfumes and cosmetics 220	👠 Shoes 110	Office supplies 50	Torches 20
Medicine 150	Walking sticks 100	🎻 Musical instruments 40	Hair dryers 10
Coins 140	Writing utensils 80	Tools 30	Binoculars 10
Various souvenirs 130	✉ Post and packing supplies 70	🐕 Pet supplies 20	Antiques 10
🔍 Sports and outdoor gear 110	Bottles, flasks and crockery 60	🚗 Cars and automotive parts 20	

Hampstead
Heath

Queen
Elizabeth
Olympic
Park

Stratford

Regent's
Park

King's Cross
St Pancras

St Paul's
Cathedral

Canary
Wharf

Trafalgar
Square

Hyde
Park

London
Eye

The
Shard

Battersea
Park

Greenwich
Park

Richmond
Park

1 4 6

The Morning Ride

Every weekday, thousands pedal to work.

Cycling has never been more popular in London. Thanks to fitness apps like Strava we can now see where millions of cyclists ride – and when. This graphic shows 6,484 journeys taken between 7 and 8 in the morning in July 2013. Routes change from blue to orange as the hour passes. Many follow quieter roads and park paths bypassed by motorists. To help channel the flow and to encourage more Londoners to trade four wheels for two, the city has named the twelve corridors below as 'cycle superhighways'.

River Thames

London City Airport

Woolwich Ferry

GREATER LONDON AUTHORITY BOUNDARY

Queen Elizabeth II Bridge

Routes of cyclists using Strava, 7–8 a.m.
Monday July 1 – Friday July 5, 2013

8 a.m.   7 a.m.

7:45   7:15

7:30

CYCLE SUPERHIGHWAYS

1	Tottenham to City	7	Merton to City
2	Bow to Aldgate	8	Wandsworth to Westminster
3	Barking to Tower Gateway	9	Hounslow to Hyde Park
4	Woolwich to London Bridge	10	Park Royal to Hyde Park
5	Lewisham to Victoria	11	West Hampstead to Marylebone
6	Penge to City	12	Muswell Hill to Angel

0   5 km

Run!

Londoners exercise at all hours.

The next four pages show the GPS tracks of 7,000 runs between 1–7 July 2013 and where people went when.

First thing in the morning, workers opted for scenic runs along the Thames, Regent's Canal and through central parks. The City of London was also popular for pre-work runs. The Greenwich foot tunnel links the skyscrapers of Canary Wharf to the green space of Greenwich Park.

WEEKDAY MORNINGS

Midnight – 10 a.m.

LEA VALLEY

Hampstead Heath

Victoria Park

Regent's Canal

KINGSLAND ROAD

Regent's Park

OXFORD STREET

CITY OF LONDON

TOWER BRIDGE

Hyde Park

South Bank

Canary Wharf

River Thames

GREENWICH FOOT TUNNEL

Gunnersbury Park

HAMMERSMITH BRIDGE

Burgess Park

Greenwich Park

Battersea Park

PUTNEY BRIDGE

Clapham Common

Brockwell Park

Dulwich Park

Richmond Park

Crystal Palace Park

0   1 km

LEA VALLEY

Hampstead
Heath

KINGSLAND ROAD

Victoria
Park

Regent's Canal

Regent's
Park

OXFORD STREET

CITY OF
LONDON

TOWER
BRIDGE

Hyde Park

South Bank

Canary
Wharf

River Thames

Gunnersbury
Park

HAMMERSMITH
BRIDGE

GREENWICH
FOOT TUNNEL

Burgess
Park

Battersea
Park

Greenwich
Park

PUTNEY
BRIDGE

Clapham
Common

0   1 km

Richmond
Park

Brockwell
Park

Dulwich
Park

During weekday lunch hours
and afternoon breaks, loops
were popular around parks
or along the north and
south banks of the Thames.
Runners from the City and
Canary Wharf also streamed
north to the Regent's Canal.
Outer parks were less busy.

Crystal
Palace Park

WEEKDAY AFTERNOONS

10 a.m. – 5 p.m.

SOURCE: STRAVA

LEA VALLEY

Hampstead
Heath

KINGSLAND ROAD

Victoria
Park

Regent's Canal

Regent's
Park

OXFORD STREET

CITY OF
LONDON

TOWER
BRIDGE

Hyde Park

South Bank

Canary
Wharf

River Thames

Gunnersbury
Park

HAMMERSMITH
BRIDGE

GREENWICH
FOOT TUNNEL

Burgess
Park

Greenwich
Park

Battersea
Park

PUTNEY
BRIDGE

Clapham
Common

Richmond
Park

0   1 km

Brockwell
Park

Dulwich
Park

Many favoured a post-work
run into the evening. All
parks were popular with
running clubs encouraging
their use. Putney Bridge
to Hammersmith Bridge
was an especially popular
Thames side circuit.

Crystal
Palace Park

WEEKDAY EVENINGS

5 p.m. – Midnight

Hampstead
Heath

LEA VALLEY

KINGSLAND ROAD

Regent's Canal

Victoria
Park

Regent's
Park

OXFORD STREET

CITY OF
LONDON

TOWER
BRIDGE

Hyde Park

South Bank

Canary
Wharf

River Thames

Gunnersbury
Park

HAMMERSMITH
BRIDGE

GREENWICH
FOOT TUNNEL

Burgess
Park

Greenwich
Park

Battersea
Park

PUTNEY
BRIDGE

——— Midnight – 10 a.m.
——— 10 a.m. – 5 p.m.
——— 5 p.m. – Midnight

Clapham
Common

0   1 km

Brockwell
Park

Dulwich
Park

The weekend saw a shift
away from pre-work routes
to suburban circuits in some
of the outer parks, notably
Hampstead Heath and
Richmond Park. A thread
of runners passed through
the Lea Valley.

Richmond
Park

Crystal
Palace Park

WEEKEND

Midnight – Midnight

Why Not Walk It?

To truly know London, walk the lines.

It took writer Mark Mason 912,384 footsteps to hike the length of every Tube line. You don't have to go quite that far to share his passion for London's streets. As Mason says, the joy of walking through London is 'about claiming the city's greatness, or at least some small part of it, for yourself.' Central London is very walkable. In many cases, it is quicker to do so than take the Tube or a bus.

When Henry Beck designed his now iconic map of the Tube network in 1931, his aim was clarity, not geographic accuracy. He expanded Central London on his map in order to accommodate its many stations and their labels. Therefore it doesn't show the distance between stops to scale. Still, his map remains so effective that it seems to make sense to take the Tube at every opportunity. Look at our map and you'll think otherwise. Charing Cross to Embankment, Leicester Square to Piccadilly Circus and Farringdon to Barbican are all short strolls. If you're still not convinced, just look at how close Lancaster Gate is to Paddington: 9 minutes on foot or 18 minutes via the Central then District lines.

Estimated walking times in minutes at an average pace of 2 metres per second
ALL TIMES ROUNDED UP TO THE NEAREST MINUTE

Station — 5 min — Station

The routes shown here are designed to follow the lines themselves. If you want real gains, try shortcuts between them. Take in the university district between Goodge Street and Russell Square or admire the City between Barbican and St Paul's.

SOURCE: OSM

HOW WE'RE DOING

Islington Has Issues

New research seeks to improve well-being by identifying who's hurting.

Since 2011, the Office for National Statistics (ONS) has asked UK residents to rate their feelings of life satisfaction, purpose, happiness and anxiety on a scale of zero to ten. In the faces to the right, we have linked each of those four questions to a different facial attribute. For example, Kensington and Chelsea shines with high life satisfaction, whereas the rest of Inner London seems lost in a mental fog.

This is not to say Londoners are *completely* miserable. Borough averages did range between six and eight for life satisfaction, purpose and happiness and between a low two and four for anxiety. Still, it's hard to ignore the average scores for the rest of the UK, where bright-eyed, smiling visages makes most Londoners seem rather tired of life by comparison. Whilst the reasons behind these differences are not yet fully understood, follow-up studies have revealed that people's perceptions of their own health, employment status and relationships mirror their sense of well-being. In other words, if you see yourself as unfit, unqualified and unlovable, there's a good chance you're unhappy.

Average personal well-being by borough
April 2012 – March 2013

Responses to the following questions ranged from 0 to 10 where 0 is 'not at all' and 10 is 'completely'. We didn't use that scale here. Instead, we rescaled London's borough averages relative to each other.

RELATIVELY HIGH

RELATIVELY LOW

Overall, how satisfied are you with your life nowadays?

Overall, to what extent do you feel the things you do in your life are worthwhile?

Overall, how happy did you feel yesterday?

Overall, how anxious did you feel yesterday?

no sweat

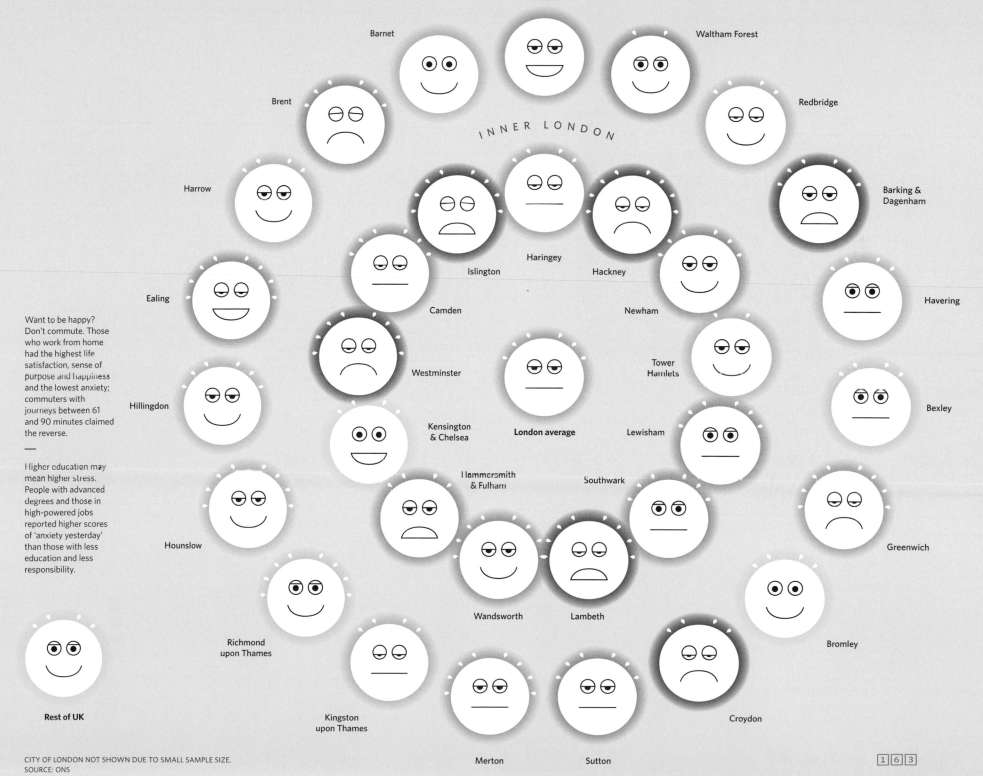

OUTER LONDON

Enfield

Barnet

Waltham Forest

Brent

Redbridge

INNER LONDON

Harrow

Barking & Dagenham

Ealing

Islington   Haringey   Hackney

Camden

Newham   Havering

Westminster

Hillingdon

Tower Hamlets

Bexley

Kensington & Chelsea   London average   Lewisham

Hammersmith & Fulham   Southwark

Hounslow

Greenwich

Wandsworth   Lambeth

Richmond upon Thames

Bromley

Rest of UK

Kingston upon Thames   Croydon

Merton   Sutton

Want to be happy? Don't commute. Those who work from home had the highest life satisfaction, sense of purpose and happiness and the lowest anxiety; commuters with journeys between 61 and 90 minutes claimed the reverse.

—

Higher education may mean higher stress. People with advanced degrees and those in high-powered jobs reported higher scores of 'anxiety yesterday' than those with less education and less responsibility.

CITY OF LONDON NOT SHOWN DUE TO SMALL SAMPLE SIZE.
SOURCE: ONS

ENFIELD

BARNET

HARROW

HARINGEY

WALTHAM
FOREST

REDBRIDGE

HAVERING

BRENT

CAMDEN

ISLINGTON

HACKNEY

BARKING
& DAGENHAM

HILLINGDON

EALING

WESTMINSTER

KENSINGTON & CHELSEA

HAMMERSMITH & FULHAM

CITY

TOWER
HAMLETS

NEWHAM

HOUNSLOW

SOUTHWARK

GREENWICH

BEXLEY

LAMBETH

WANDSWORTH

LEWISHAM

RICHMOND
UPON THAMES

KINGSTON
UPON
THAMES

MERTON

BROMLEY

SUTTON

CROYDON

0   5 km

High housing prices may be
pushing those on the lowest
wages to the outer boroughs
as the wealthier move in.
Gentrification does not
offer a solution to citywide
poverty; it simply moves the
challenge on to other areas
of the capital.

Deprivation by decile
2010

MOST DEPRIVED

LEAST DEPRIVED

'It was the best of times, it was the worst of times...'

In 1854, five years before Charles Dickens wrote the first line of *A Tale of Two Cities*, the physician John Snow made a map. With cholera inexplicably ravaging West London, Snow set out to find its source. By plotting the locations of its victims, he noticed that many clustered near a particular water pump on Broad Street in Soho.

'The result of the inquiry,' he wrote, 'is that there has been no particular outbreak or prevalence of cholera in this part of London except among the persons who were in the habit of drinking the water of the above-mentioned pump well.' Not only did his map save lives, it kick-started the science of epidemiology and the notion that maps and graphics can be agents for the greater good.

In the light of such advances, it is surprising that it took thirty years before someone applied these techniques to the very poverty Dickens wrote about. That someone was Charles Booth. Having made a fortune in shipping, Booth invested it on the most comprehensive social survey of London ever undertaken. He then visualized his findings in a series of detailed 'poverty maps' published in 1889 (see p. 25). Given their simplicity – strips of colour drawn over an off-the-shelf map of the city – it is easy to overlook that each one required a visit from Booth or his colleagues to assess a street's 'social condition'. This painstaking work illustrated London's class spectrum from wealth through to destitution and offered the first definitive map of where Londoners were most in need.

Times have changed, but London's poverty remains largely concentrated in the East End. The persistent have/have-not divide casts a shadow over many of the graphics in this chapter. On the left, we show a contemporary measure of poverty called the Index of Multiple Deprivation. It depicts the most (red) and least deprived (green) areas of London based on their inhabitants' education, income, employment, health, experience of crime, housing accessibility and living environment. For many in the reddest areas, daily life demands a series of fundamental decisions about sourcing your next meal, your next rent payment, your child's school uniform. The Index is widely used by those seeking to rid Londoners of this centuries-old reality, but in comparison to its Victorian predecessor, it offers little in the way of visual innovation.

So if Booth were alive today, what would he do? We'd like to think he'd get data scientists, computer programmers, designers, policy makers and other volunteers together to mine any number of datasets posted online by charities and the government. Who knows what life-saving maps they might generate? Better still, he might offer training to those without the Internet (see pp. 194–5), empowering them to access the same open health and crime data we've visualized in this chapter. Data literally offer strength in numbers. The more of us who can use them, the stronger we will be.

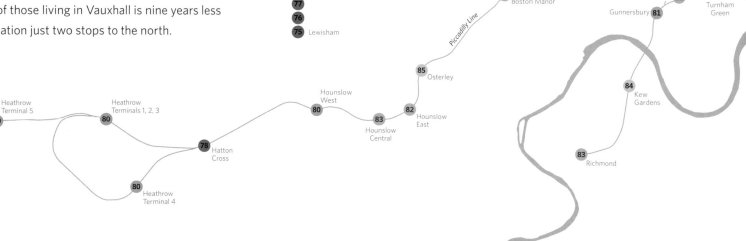

Lives on the Line

'Mind the Gap' in life expectancy.

To see inequalities across London in the twenty-first century, look no further than the Jubilee Line. For every two stops east between Westminster and Canning Town, the London Health Observatory estimates that life expectancy of local residents drops one year. The Tube therefore acts as a new measuring tool for the city. Pick any two stations that matter to you and see how values fluctuate between them. For example, the life expectancy of those living in Vauxhall is nine years less than that of those living near Victoria Station just two stops to the north.

Life expectancy at birth +/- 3 years
2006-2010 (rolling average)

91 Knightsbridge
90
89
88
87
86
85
84
83 Female Citywide Average
82
81
80
79 Male Citywide Average
78
77
76
75 Lewisham

Underground
Overground
Docklands Light Rail

◯ No data

SOURCE: LONDON HEALTH PROGRAMMES

Though the gap between Londoners' life expectancies is stark, the overall picture is improving. Between 2003 and 2013, premature mortality rates fell by around a third. They're now below the England average.

239 instances
restaurant

café
227 instances

What's to Eat?

Your options depend on where you live.

The Food Standards Agency database contains the name and address of every food outlet in London (with the exception of Greenwich). We overlaid these on our poverty map (see p. 164) to see the most frequently used words in the names of 1,680 restaurants, canteens, takeaways and sandwich shops from the richest and poorest parts of London. As we show here, you would struggle to find fried chicken on your plate in Mayfair or haute French cuisine in Poplar, but fish and pizza are universally enjoyed whatever your means.

Top 150 words used in café or restaurant names in London's most (top 10%) and least (bottom 10%) deprived areas, 2014

50 instances

20

5

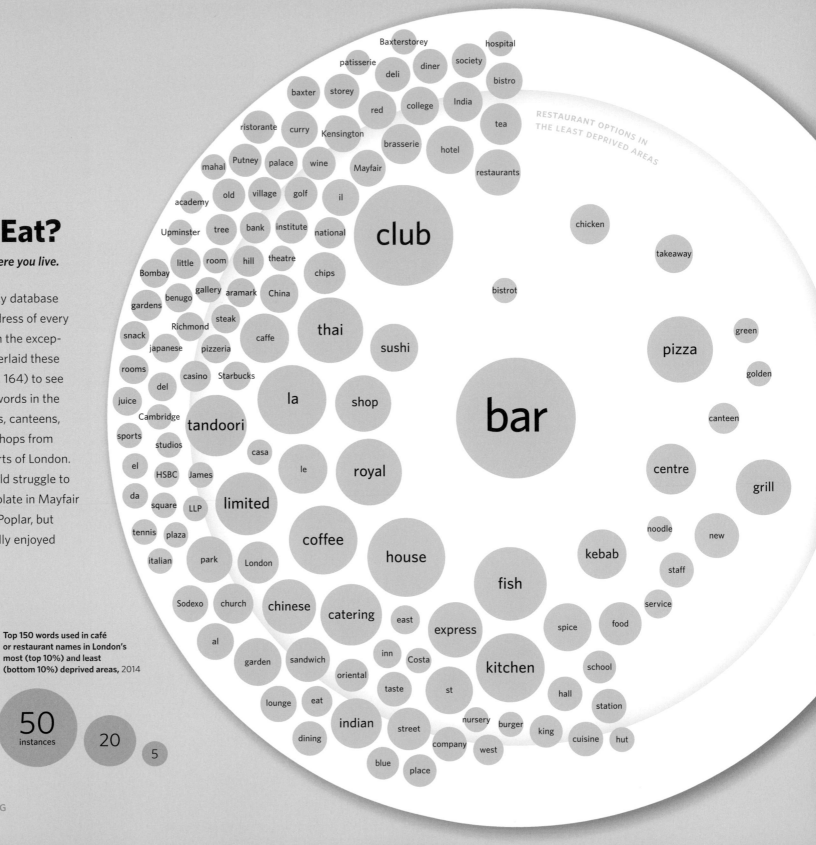

RESTAURANT OPTIONS IN THE LEAST DEPRIVED AREAS

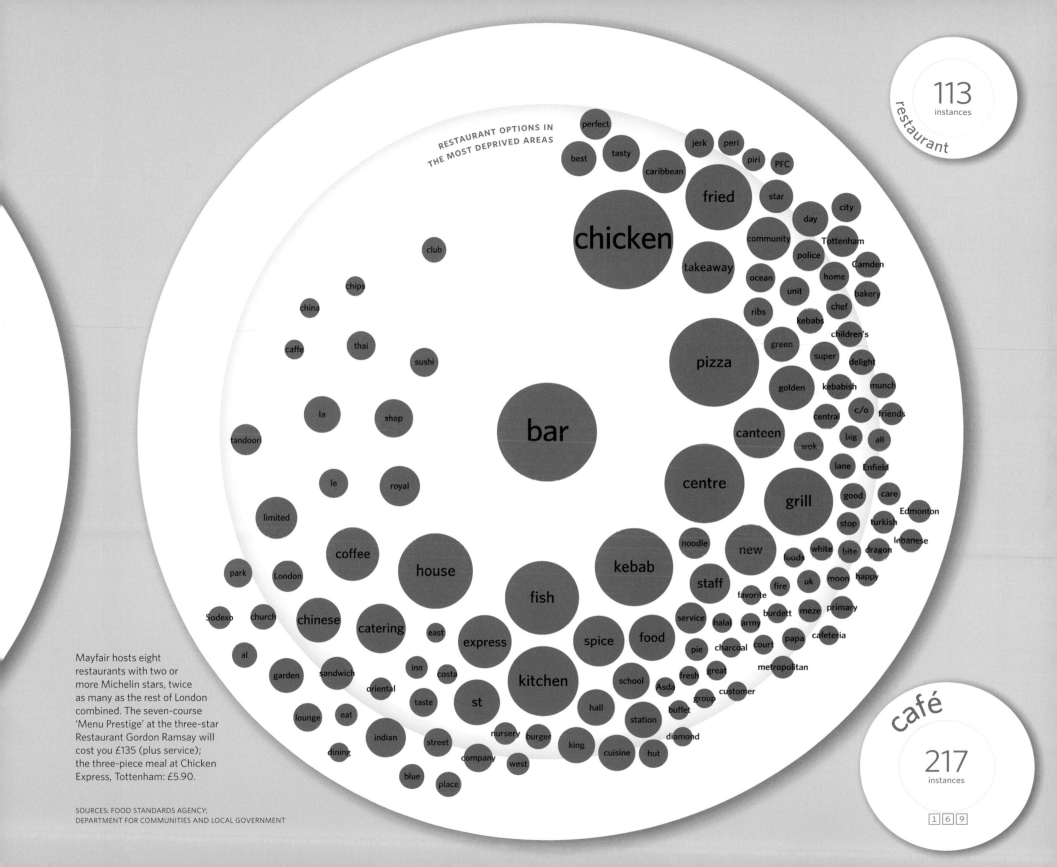

RESTAURANT OPTIONS IN
THE MOST DEPRIVED AREAS

113 instances
restaurant

café
217 instances

1 6 9

Mayfair hosts eight restaurants with two or more Michelin stars, twice as many as the rest of London combined. The seven-course 'Menu Prestige' at the three-star Restaurant Gordon Ramsay will cost you £135 (plus service); the three-piece meal at Chicken Express, Tottenham: £5.90.

SOURCES: FOOD STANDARDS AGENCY;
DEPARTMENT FOR COMMUNITIES AND LOCAL GOVERNMENT

The Shape of Obesity

Where wallets contract, waistlines expand.

Some of the heaviest children in England live in London. In order to show where, we expanded or contracted each borough to reflect the extent to which children living there are more or less obese than the English average (18.9%). The geography may be distorted, but the inequalities are not. In more deprived areas like Newham and Tower Hamlets – where the obesity rate stretches above 25% – the bulge threatens to burst the buckle off the Thames. Compare this to wealthier boroughs like Richmond and Kingston upon Thames, where rates below 15% shrink their boundaries to thin lines.

Percentage of 10–11-year-olds classified obese, 2012–13

- More than 25%
- 20–25

English average — Less than 20%
18.9%

Body Mass Index (BMI) is the measure used to determine a healthy weight. It divides a person's weight in kilograms by the square of their height in metres. In population statistics, children whose BMI is at or above the 95th percentile are classified as obese.

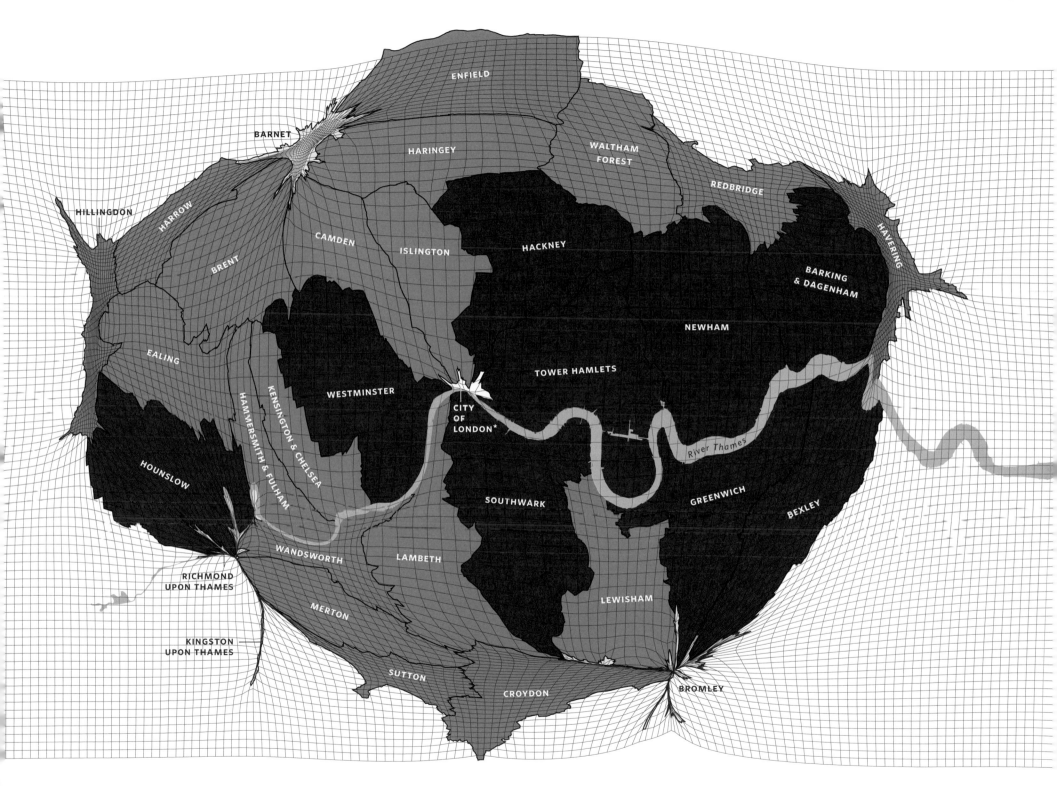

HILLINGDON

BARNET

ENFIELD

HARROW

HARINGEY

WALTHAM FOREST

BRENT

CAMDEN

ISLINGTON

HACKNEY

REDBRIDGE

HAVERING

EALING

WESTMINSTER

KENSINGTON & CHELSEA

HAMMERSMITH & FULHAM

CITY OF LONDON*

TOWER HAMLETS

NEWHAM

BARKING & DAGENHAM

HOUNSLOW

River Thames

SOUTHWARK

GREENWICH

BEXLEY

WANDSWORTH

LAMBETH

RICHMOND UPON THAMES

MERTON

LEWISHAM

KINGSTON UPON THAMES

SUTTON

CROYDON

BROMLEY

Causes of Death

We're not dying like we used to.

Three and a half centuries ago, a haberdasher-turned-demographer named John Graunt began to wonder how we die. For thirty years, he tallied the causes of death in London before publishing them in his *Bills of Mortality* in 1662. His 'Table of Casualties' inspired ours, but it looked far different from the one you see to the right. For one, in 1650, the top cause of death was 'Consumption, and Cough'. Today, heart disease leads the list – and no one dies from 'Teeth and Worms', 'Itch' or 'Wolf'.

By adding gender and borough data to the table, we can now see patterns Graunt would have envied. Note how, in most boroughs, the death rates for their ten leading causes have gone down apart from dementia and Alzheimer's, which have climbed into the top ten for women in more boroughs than men. Men, however, are more likely to die from liver disease. In case you were wondering, that's how Graunt died.

To aid your exploration, we've highlighted the boroughs with the top three death rates for each cause. Boroughs and causes were ordered by total death rate in 2012.

Age-standardized rates per 100,000 people for each gender's ten leading causes of death, 2001-2012

Top 3 boroughs per cause
Higher than 2001
No change
Lower than 2001
-------- No rate calculated

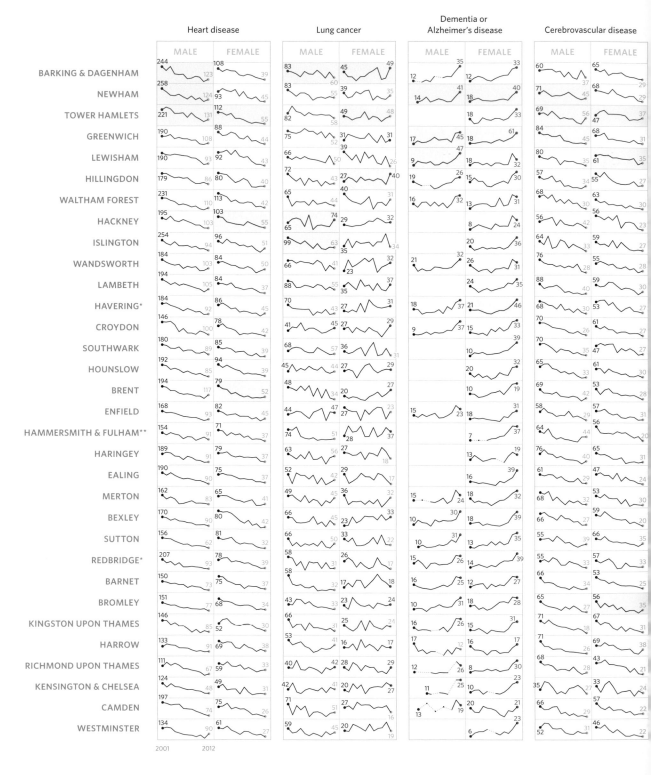

SOURCE: ONS

Chronic lower respiratory diseases | Influenza or pneumonia | Colon cancer | Heart failure and ill-defined heart disease | Lymphoma or Leukemia | Breast cancer | Prostate cancer | Liver disease | Urinary system diseases | Suicide

| MALE | FEMALE | MALE | FEMALE | MALE | FEMALE | MALE | FEMALE | MALE | FEMALE | FEMALE | MALE | MALE | FEMALE | MALE |

*ONLY 18 CAUSES SHOWN. TOP MALE CAUSES INCLUDE AORTIC ANEURYSM (HAVERING) AND URINARY SYSTEM DISEASES (REDBRIDGE).
**21 CAUSES SHOWN BECAUSE OF A TIE. URINARY SYSTEM DISEASES AND LYMPHOMA CAUSED THE SAME TOTAL NUMBER OF DEATHS IN FEMALES.

1 7 3

Quit Dates

Londoners are trying to stop smoking.

Smoking continues to be the leading cause of preventable deaths in the UK. Come New Year's Day, thousands resolve to kick the habit with the help of National Health Service (NHS) Stop Smoking Services. Many fail. Of the half a million Londoners who set a quit date between 2008 and 2013, 48% reported that they had quit at their 4-week follow up. After measuring the carbon monoxide levels in their blood, the number of confirmed ex-smokers had in fact dropped to 34%.

Quitting is hard. On average, it takes seven to ten attempts to succeed. Google searches for 'quit smoking' spike on Mondays, so experts are encouraging smokers to make weekly resolutions instead of annual ones. That's fifty-one more chances to change.

Number of self-reported quitters vs. quitters confirmed by carbon monoxide testing by quarter
April 2008 – January 2013

SOURCES: HEALTH & SOCIAL CARE INFORMATION CENTRE; NHS STOP SMOKING SERVICES

16,600
self-reported
quitters

16,800

15,000

10,950
confirmed by carbon
monoxide testing

12,000

10,000
self-reported
quitters

5,000

2008
98,600 set a quit date
46,400 reported quitting
32,600 confirmed

2009
107,500 set a quit date
49,500 reported quitting
34,000 confirmed

April   July   October   January   April   July   October   Jan

16,800

15,800

15,500

12,200

11,250

11,300

10,000

5,000

October 2012
The NHS launches Stoptober, a nationwide 28-day smoking challenge. Those who give up cigarettes for four weeks are more likely to stay smoke-free. The average participant saved £141 in cigarette money – and a week of their life.

2010
108,500 set a quit date
50,900 reported quitting
35,200 confirmed

2011
108,500 set a quit date
53,600 reported quitting
37,600 confirmed

2012
100,500 set a quit date
53,000 reported quitting
37,400 confirmed

April   July   October   January   April   July   October   January   April   July   October

Pill Boxes

London's prescriptions indicate its health concerns.

Over the course of a year, National Health Service general practitioners prescribe more than a billion items in England. Doctors in London contribute 116 million to this total. The graphic on the right shows the 120 most-prescribed drugs in the capital, sized by number of prescriptions and grouped by general purpose. (Several drugs have multiple uses.) Heart disease, hypertension and cholesterol are the most frequently treated conditions.

Darker shades of green indicate higher prices. Branded drugs such as Atorvastatin are often more expensive than generic varieties, so they tend to be prescribed far less. For £1.40, Simvastatin offers a much cheaper means of reducing cholesterol and the risks of heart attack and stroke. In fact, for every ailment listed, there's an option for ten pounds or less.

Number of prescriptions ———
Average cost per item ———

120 most prescribed drugs by amount, purpose and item cost
March 2013 – February 2014

AVERAGE COST (£)

- 0–10
- 10–20
- 20–30
- 30–40
- 40–50
- 50–60

Heart disease and hypertension

Amlodipine
3,517,000 prescriptions
£1.42 each

Ramipril
2,872,000
1.61

Bisoprolol Fumarate
1,679,000
1.53

Simvastatin
4,525,000
1.40

Bendro-flumethiazide
1,550,000
1.16

Losartan Potassium
991,000
2.07

Doxazosin Mesilate
858,000
3.70

Isosorbide Mononitrate
479,000 / 7.77

Omeprazole
2,901,000
2.34

Perindopril Erbumine
468,000 / 2.31

Lisinopril
977,000
1.63

Indapamide
453,000
7.61

Enalapril Maleate
317,000
1.85

Diltiazem
306,000
9.07

Furosemide
1,253,000
1.01

Atenolol
926,000
1.19

Irbesartan
353,000
3.40

Nifedipine
287,000
8.78

Felodipine
254,000
6.97

Propranolol
317,000
7.29

Spironolactone
271,000
1.86

Nicorandil
190,000
4.53

Painkiller

Paracetamol
2,448,000
2.89

Ibuprofen
865,000
3.25

Naproxen
706,000
3.18

Co-Dydramol
550,000
3.15

Other Emollient Preparations
1,703,000
5.92

Gabapentin
390,000
5.93

Diclofenac
254,000
5.28

Tramadol Hydrochloride
745,000
5.38

Co-Codamol
1,323,000
4.65

Pregabalin
386,000
59.96

Piroxicam
210,000
4.12

Hydrocortisone
767,000
3.07

Codeine
195,000
3.67

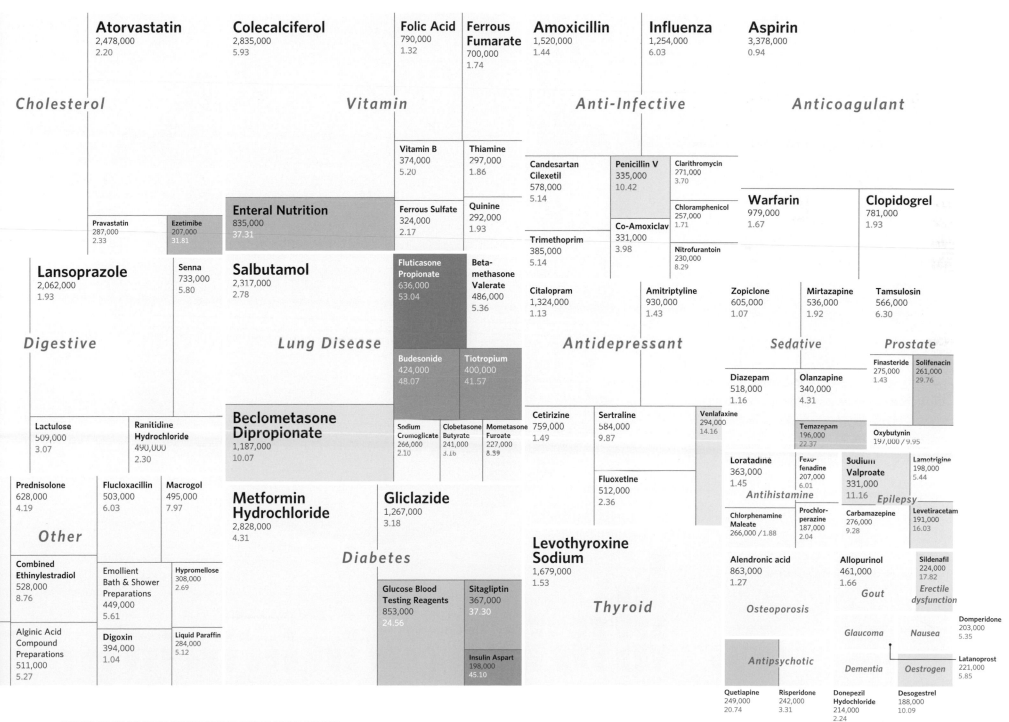

Atorvastatin
2,478,000
2.20

Colecalciferol
2,835,000
5.93

Folic Acid
790,000
1.32

Ferrous Fumarate
700,000
1.74

Amoxicillin
1,520,000
1.44

Influenza
1,254,000
6.03

Aspirin
3,378,000
0.94

Cholesterol

Vitamin

Anti-Infective

Anticoagulant

Vitamin B
374,000
5.20

Thiamine
297,000
1.86

Candesartan Cilexetil
578,000
5.14

Penicillin V
335,000
10.42

Clarithromycin
271,000
3.70

Pravastatin
287,000
2.33

Ezetimibe
207,000
31.81

Enteral Nutrition
835,000
37.31

Ferrous Sulfate
324,000
2.17

Quinine
292,000
1.93

Chloramphenicol
257,000
1.71

Warfarin
979,000
1.67

Clopidogrel
781,000
1.93

Co-Amoxiclav
331,000
3.98

Senna
733,000
5.80

Trimethoprim
385,000
5.14

Nitrofurantoin
230,000
8.29

Lansoprazole
2,062,000
1.93

Salbutamol
2,317,000
2.78

Fluticasone Propionate
636,000
53.04

Beta-methasone Valerate
486,000
5.36

Citalopram
1,324,000
1.13

Amitriptyline
930,000
1.43

Zopiclone
605,000
1.07

Mirtazapine
536,000
1.92

Tamsulosin
566,000
6.30

Digestive

Lung Disease

Antidepressant

Sedative

Prostate

Budesonide
424,000
48.07

Tiotropium
400,000
41.57

Diazepam
518,000
1.16

Olanzapine
340,000
4.31

Finasteride
275,000
1.43

Solifenacin
261,000
29.76

Lactulose
509,000
3.07

Ranitidine Hydrochloride
490,000
2.30

Cetirizine
759,000
1.49

Sertraline
584,000
9.87

Venlafaxine
294,000
14.16

Temazepam
196,000
22.37

Oxybutynin
197,000 / 9.95

Beclometasone Dipropionate
1,187,000
10.07

Sodium Cromoglicate
266,000
2.10

Clobetasone Butyrate
241,000
3.16

Mometasone Furoate
227,000
8.39

Loratadine
363,000
1.45

Fexo-fenadine
207,000
6.01

Sodium Valproate
331,000
11.16

Lamotrigine
198,000
5.44

Epilepsy

Antihistamine

Prednisolone
628,000
4.19

Flucloxacillin
503,000
6.03

Macrogol
495,000
7.97

Fluoxetine
512,000
2.36

Chlorphenamine Maleate
266,000 / 1.88

Prochlor-perazine
187,000
2.04

Carbamazepine
276,000
9.28

Levetiracetam
191,000
16.03

Metformin Hydrochloride
2,828,000
4.31

Gliclazide
1,267,000
3.18

Alendronic acid
863,000
1.27

Allopurinol
461,000
1.66

Sildenafil
224,000
17.82

Erectile dysfunction

Other

Diabetes

Levothyroxine Sodium
1,679,000
1.53

Osteoporosis

Gout

Combined Ethinylestradiol
528,000
8.76

Emollient Bath & Shower Preparations
449,000
5.61

Hypromellose
308,000
2.69

Glucose Blood Testing Reagents
853,000
24.56

Sitagliptin
367,000
37.30

Domperidone
203,000
5.35

Glaucoma

Nausea

Thyroid

Alginic Acid Compound Preparations
511,000
5.27

Digoxin
394,000
1.04

Liquid Paraffin
284,000
5.12

Insulin Aspart
198,000
45.10

Antipsychotic

Dementia

Oestrogen

Latanoprost
221,000
5.85

Quetiapine
249,000
20.74

Risperidone
242,000
3.31

Donepezil Hydrochloride
214,000
2.24

Desogestrel
188,000
10.09

SOURCES: HEALTH AND SOCIAL CARE INFORMATION CENTRE; LETTY DORMANDY

Call 999

Drunks are an emergency the city could do without.

9-9-9, the world's first emergency phone service went live in London on 1 July 1937. It was an instant success. In the first week, dispatchers handled 1,300 calls. They'd be pleased to know that seventy-six years later, in 2013, the service responded to 1.1 million calls. They might not be so keen to learn that 32,500 of them were for incapacitated binge-drinkers (see chart).

Alcohol-related hospital admissions cost the National Health Service £3.5 billion a year. To relieve accident and emergency departments, London Ambulance Service began running 'booze buses' in 2005. These specially outfitted ambulances can transport five patients at a time to alcohol recovery centres in Central London. There, patients receive water, a bed and advice on how to drink responsibly.

DECEMBER — 2,900 reports — 95
The booze bus extends its hours for 'Black Friday' and the heavy party days before Christmas.

JANUARY — 2,100 — 69
London sobers up with a 'Dry January' after ringing in the New Year.

FEBRUARY — 2,300 — 81

MARCH — 2,700 — 88

NOVEMBER — 2,600 — 87

OCTOBER — 2,800 — 91 reports per day

APRIL — 2,500 — 83

100 reports

Binge-drinking peaks in hot summer months. In 2013, there were 100 alcohol-related calls a day between June and September.

SEPTEMBER — 2,500 — 83

MAY — 2,800 — 89

AUGUST — 3,100 — 101

JULY — 3,100 — 100

JUNE — 3,000 — 101

1,000 2,000 3,000

Binge drinking by month, 2013

Boroughs with the most binge-drinking incidents, 2013

 = 300 reports

With its many pubs, clubs and restaurants, Westminster reports the highest number of binge-drinking incidents, more than double the next drunkest boroughs, Camden and Lambeth.

Borough average

Westminster   Camden   Lambeth   Southwark   Hackney   Croydon   Tower Hamlets   Newham   Islington   Wandsworth

By comparison, this chart shows a much smaller number of 999 reports. In 2013, paramedics attended 1,429 call-outs involving injuries caused by knives (orange); 431 caused by large animals, many of which were dogs (yellow line); and 214 caused by guns (black). Of course, not all victims call 999. By the police's count, there were twice as many: 3,200 crimes involving knife injuries, 830 dog bites and 312 crimes where a gun was fired.

Notice how the overall shape of the injury wedges matches the wedges for binge-drinking. All increased during the hot summer months and in March, October and December. For more correlations between alcohol and violence, turn the page.

DECEMBER   JANUARY
NOVEMBER   FEBRUARY
OCTOBER   MARCH
Knife injuries
Injured by animal
Gunshots
100 reports   1,000
SEPTEMBER   APRIL
AUGUST   MAY
JULY   JUNE

Injury-related incidents by cause by month, 2013

Boroughs with the most incidents involving guns or knives, 2013

 = 10 reports

Ambulances travelled to Lambeth for 112 knife injuries and 17 gun wounds in 2013, more than any other borough. Five of the other boroughs with more than seventy victims were also in Inner London.

Borough average

Lambeth   Newham   Lewisham   Southwark   Hackney   Haringey   Croydon   Ealing   Tower Hamlets   Brent

Flashpoints

Where intoxication increases, violent crime flares up.

The website *police.uk* maps every reported crime down to street level. Using these data, researcher Matt Ashby from University College London's Department of Security and Crime Science identified the violent crime hotspots you see on the right. Between April 2012 and March 2013, nearly 80% of London's streets experienced no such crimes (grey). Those that did, he coloured from more (red) to less (yellow).

As Ashby puts it on his blog, *lesscrime.info*, 'Central London is in a class of its own.' More than 2,000 violent crimes – which include murder, assault, harassment, kidnapping as well as all sex offences – were recorded around Soho and Leicester Square. Shoreditch, Brixton, Camden Town and Whitechapel round out the top five. This is to be expected, although no less acceptable, given the number of people passing through these areas at night, fuelled on alcohol from the many clubs and bars (see pp. 178–9). Further out, violent crime gathers along arterial roads and around suburban town centres. Some of these, such as Romford and Croydon, have given the rest of their borough a bad name, which, as Ashby says, 'must be galling if you live in ultra-leafy Hornchurch or Shirley'.

DODGY AREAS

Over the course of a year, more than 750 violent crimes were reported within a one-kilometre radius of these twenty areas. Seven of the top ten are in Central London.

1. Soho and Leicester Square
2. Shoreditch
3. Brixton
4. Camden Town
5. Whitechapel
6. Hackney
7. Ladbroke Grove and Kensal Town
8. Elephant and Castle
9. Peckham
10. Croydon
11. Archway
12. Stratford
13. Shepherd's Bush
14. King's Cross and Angel
15. Dalston
16. Edgware Road and Marble Arch
17. Poplar
18. Woolwich
19. Kingston
20. Wood Green

Violent crimes
April 2012 – March 2013

MORE CRIME

LESS CRIME

0   5 km

Top Crimes

Watch your wallet in Westminster.

Tourists take note. Things have a habit of disappearing in London, especially amidst the many shops, pubs and attractions in the centre. In 2012–13, the Metropolitan police (MPS) responded to 37,000 thefts in Westminster alone, three times as many as the next borough. While theft was prevalent in all boroughs, when we focused on the most common crimes in 200 metre by 200 metre areas, new patterns emerged (see right). Pockets of violent and vehicle crime (yellow, orange) appeared, transitioning to a ring of burglaries (purple) in more residential areas. We excluded the 341,000 anti-social behaviour reports, which included 'crimes' like loitering, littering, spitting, begging, door-slamming, loud music, abusive language, fare evasion, fireworks and barking dogs. If we hadn't, they would have covered the whole map!

CRIME'S DECLINE

Though crime rates have dropped in every borough, fear has not. According to an MPS survey, 54% of Newham residents said they were worried about crime, compared to 15% in Kingston. Both experience fewer crimes than London's top three.

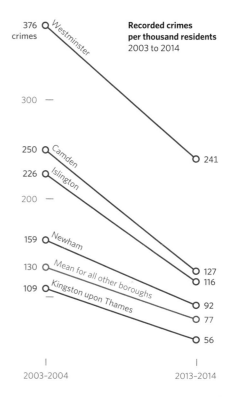

Recorded crimes per thousand residents 2003 to 2014

376 crimes — Westminster → 241

250 — Camden → 127

226 — Islington → 116

159 — Newham → 92

130 — Mean for all other boroughs → 77

109 — Kingston upon Thames → 56

2003–2004   2013–2014

ENFIELD

BARNET

HARROW

HARINGEY

WALTHAM
FOREST

REDBRIDGE

HAVERING

HILLINGDON

BRENT

CAMDEN

ISLINGTON

HACKNEY

BARKING
& DAGENHAM

NEWHAM

EALING

HAMMERSMITH & FULHAM

KENSINGTON & CHELSEA

WESTMINSTER

CITY

TOWER
HAMLETS

River Thames

HOUNSLOW

WANDSWORTH

LAMBETH

SOUTHWARK

GREENWICH

BEXLEY

LEWISHAM

RICHMOND
UPON THAMES

MERTON

KINGSTON
UPON
THAMES

0   5 km

BROMLEY

SUTTON

CROYDON

**Top crime per
200 x 200 metre area**
2012–13

- Theft or shoplifting
- Violent crime
- Vehicle crime
- Burglary
- Criminal damage or arson
- No single top crime
- Other

SOURCES: POLICE.UK; METROPOLITAN POLICE SERVICE (CHART)

You Can't Hide

Day or night, police helicopters find suspects on the run.

Altitude isn't their only advantage. The airborne officers can see in the dark. What may seem like great camouflage to a suspect in a garden at 2 a.m. is clearer than day to the helicopter's thermal-imaging sensor, where a warm body contrasts like black ink on a white page. The crew then uses radios and a 30-million candle-power spotlight to guide ground units to the suspect.

The Air Support Unit averages 275 flight hours a month between its three choppers: India 99, 98 and 97. Crews change shifts twice a day: once in the evening and again before criminals wake up. Here, we plotted every mission flown in July 2013, coloured by purpose. The silhouettes indicate when they successfully detained a suspect or located a missing person. When not conducting searches, you may see the helicopter hovering above concerts, demonstrations and sporting events. Its 360-degree video camera provides a vital aerial feed to crowd control officers on the scene. The unit's 100,000 Twitter followers know @MPSinthesky best for another purpose: spectacular photos of the city.

Choppers can fly from their base in Lippitts Hill to Westminster Bridge in six minutes. They don't always start so far away. By conducting routine patrols across the city, the helicopters put themselves in position to respond to incidents in any borough.

Most frequent destinations
July 2013

30 flights
20
10

Helicopter flights by task type
July 2013

Search for suspect
Vehicle follow or pursuit
Search for missing person
Photo or video tasks
Crowd control
Tactical support
Other

 Suspect detained

 Missing person found

9:00   10:00   11:00   Noon   1:00   2:00   3:00   4:00   5:00   6:00   7:00   8:00   9:00   10:00   11:00   Midnight

SHIFT CHANGE

1 6 JULY
At midnight, @MPSinthesky tweeted a thermal image of a concert at Wembley Stadium. Later, they posted one of Battersea Power Station 'all lit up'. Such images keep a strong Twitter following, which the crew sometimes enlists to help locate missing persons.

2 5 JULY
The unit's longest day of the month kept them airborne for sixteen hours. After a series of late-night searches, the day crew lifted at 7:30 a.m. for a long stretch of crowd control above the first day of the British Summer Time festival in Hyde Park.

3 18 JULY
Often when one task ends, another begins. Between 4 and 6:30 p.m., the helicopter located a suspect in Westminster; made vehicle stops in Hackney; found missing persons in Haringey and Bexley; and gave tactical support for a coach fire on the M25.

4 19 JULY
Thirty-seven flights – including car chases, roof searches, lost persons, photos of Lord's Cricket Ground and support for firefighters battling a heat-wave-induced grass fire – are all in a day's work for London's chopper coppers.

We obtained these data through a Freedom of Information request (see pp. 22–3). Not all flight records were shared because to do so would 'allow interested parties to gain an upper hand and awareness of policing decisions used to safeguard national security'.

SOURCE: METROPOLITAN POLICE SERVICE

**London Fire Brigade
callouts for fires by station**
November 2010 – October 2011

Station status
Open
Closed January 2014

In response to budget cuts,
ten fire stations – including
Clerkenwell, London's oldest
– closed in January 2014.

Enfield
Barnet
Southgate
Edmonton
Chingford
Mill Hill
Woodford
Hainault
Stanmore
Finchley
Romford
Harold Hill
Harrow
Hendon
Tottenham
Walthamstow
Ruislip
Hornsey
Ilford
Dagenham
Hornchurch
Northolt
Wembley
West Hampstead
Stoke
Newington
Leyton
Leytonstone
Holloway
Kentish Town
Homerton
Stratford
Hillingdon
Willesden
Belsize
Islington
Barking
Park Royal
Kingsland
Bow
North
Kensington
Euston
Shoreditch
Bethnal
Green
East Ham
Paddington
Clerkenwell
Plaistow
Soho
Whitechapel
Poplar
Wennington
Dowgate
Shadwell
Ealing
Kensington
Silvertown
Southall
Acton
Knightsbridge
Southwark
Millwall
Hammersmith
Westminster
Dockhead
Woolwich
Plumstead
Erith
Hayes
Chelsea
Lambeth
Old Kent Road
Deptford
East Greenwich
Heathrow
Fulham
Peckham
Greenwich
Bexley
Heston
New Cross
Chiswick
Battersea
Richmond
Clapham
Brixton
Lewisham
Eltham
Feltham
Wandsworth
Lee
Green
Forest Hill
Twickenham
Downham
Sidcup
Kingston
Tooting
West Norwood
New Malden
Mitcham
Norbury
Beckenham
Bromley
Surbiton
Woodside
Orpington
Sutton
Croydon
Wallington
Addington
Purley
Biggin Hill

0   5 km

Sound the Alarm!

Life is never quiet for the London Fire Brigade.

Lighting up the city like an array of fireworks, each of the 30,354 lines to the left connects a fire station to a blaze between November 2010 and October 2011. These bursts form only part of the year's display, however, since only 22% of the total call outs went to actual fires (see below). False alarms triggered by automatic systems at office blocks, hospitals, universities and airports accounted for much of the rest. Additionally, firefighters were often called to provide 'special services', such as freeing people from lifts (9,482 incidents), rescuing animals (698) or assisting the increasing number of people 'stuck or trapped in objects' like handcuffs or toilet seats (416). These often avoidable situations – each costing taxpayers £290 on average – can steal crews away from genuine emergencies. In 2013, the Brigade took to Twitter using the #fiftyshadesofred hashtag to highlight some of the most ridiculous incidents they have ever attended (see right). To avoid being featured, heed their advice: 'If you use handcuffs, always keep the keys handy.'

#FIFTYSHADESOFRED

The Brigade attended more than 1,300 'removal of object' incidents between 2010 and 2013, including:

491 rings stuck on fingers

379 people trapped in or under machinery

79 trapped in handcuffs

36 impaled on objects

18 children with heads stuck in potties

17 children with fingers stuck in toys

9 hands caught in shredders or blenders

9 rings stuck on penises

FIRES **FALSE ALARMS** **SPECIAL SERVICES**

London Fire Brigade callouts by type
November 2010 – October 2011

- None
- 1–9
- 10–19
- 20–39
- 40–59
- 60–79
- 80–99
- 100 or more

SOURCE: LONDON FIRE BRIGADE

WHAT WE LIKE

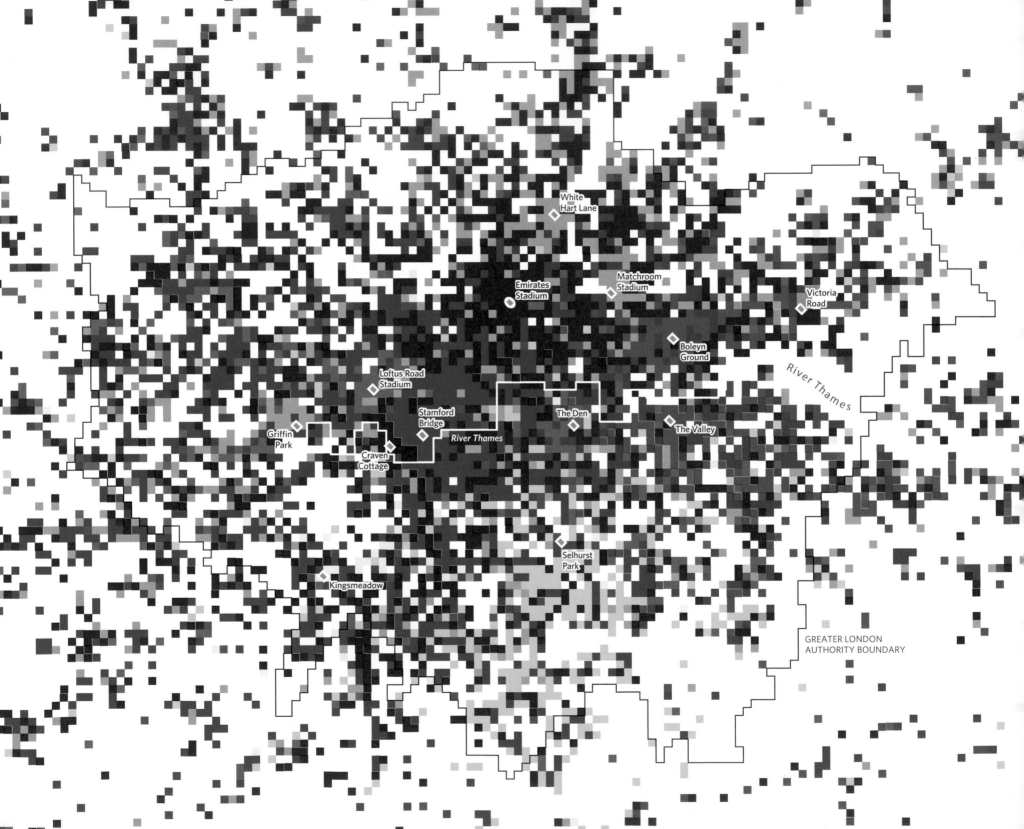

White
Hart Lane

Matchroom
Stadium

Emirates
Stadium

Victoria
Road

Boleyn
Ground

River Thames

Loftus Road
Stadium

Stamford
Bridge

The Den

The Valley

Griffin
Park

River Thames

Craven
Cottage

Selhurst
Park

Kingsmeadow

GREATER LONDON
AUTHORITY BOUNDARY

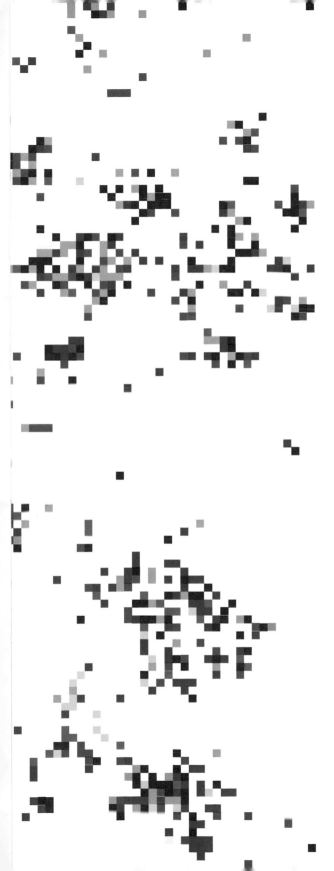

The Football Tribes

Win or lose, fans of London clubs voice their allegiance on Twitter.

On 22 March 2014, the Chelsea Blues crushed their red rivals 6–0 in a game neither club will soon forget. Arsenal fans took to Twitter to bemoan the loss ('Utterly, woefully, hideously execrable. #afc') while #carefree Chelsea beamed with pride ('There's only one team in London!' #cfc).

In fact, there are thirteen professional football clubs in London. Here, we divided the city into squares, each coloured by the club with the most tweeted hashtag in that area. Taken together, the squares form a mosaic of football loyalties. Chelsea (dark blue) and Arsenal (red) – the London clubs with the most titles in Premier League history (3 each) – dominate on both sides of the Thames; tweets for the eleven other clubs mostly prevail near their grounds.

Chelsea finished the season ahead of Arsenal in the League and in the Twittersphere. The recent #ChampionsOfEurope out-tweeted the Gunners 22,000–19,000. On this map, blue is the colour, indeed.

London's football clubs by popularity on Twitter
August 2013 – May 2014

Each square measures 500 x 500 metres.

A square's colour indicates the football club with the most tweeted hashtag in that area.

PREMIER LEAGUE

■ **CHELSEA**	■ **ARSENAL**	■ **TOTTENHAM**
Stamford Bridge	*Emirates Stadium*	*White Hart Lane*
WINS / LOSSES / DRAWS		
2013–14 record: **25-7-6** *(3rd place)*	2013–14 record: **24-7-7** *(4th)*	2013–14 record: **21-6-11** *(6th)*

■ **CRYSTAL PALACE**	■ **WEST HAM**	■ **FULHAM**
Selhurst Park	*Boleyn Ground*	*Craven Cottage*
2013–14 record: **13-6-19** *(11th)*	2013–14 record: **11-7-20** *(13th)*	2013–14 record: **9-5-24** *(19th)*

FOOTBALL LEAGUE CHAMPIONSHIP

- ■ Queens Park Rangers
- ■ Charlton Athletic
- ■ Millwall

LEAGUE ONE

- ■ Brentford
- ■ Leyton Orient

LEAGUE TWO

- ■ Dagenham & Redbridge
- AFC Wimbledon

SOURCES: TWITTER; GUY LANSLEY AND MUHAMMAD ADNAN, UNIVERSITY COLLEGE LONDON

Regent's Canal

London
Zoo

King's Cross
St Pancras

Regent's Canal

Regent's Park

Lord's
Cricket
Ground

Little
Venice

SHOREDITCH

Paddington
Station

OXFORD STREET

SOHO

St Paul's
Cathedral

Hyde Park

Trafalgar
Square

Tower
of London

The Serpentine

Tate
Modern

Borough
Market

THE MALL

London
Eye

River Thames

Buckingham
Palace

Royal
Albert Hall

Palace
of Westminster

Natural
History
Museum

Elephant and Castle

Battersea
Park

0   1 km

Photogenic Features

Millions of Flickr users capture London's best side.

A sleepy tiger, a blue whale, the Queen's Guards and the arc of the London Eye. To get these shots, leave your guidebook at home and head to spots on this map. Researchers Alexander Kachkaev and Jo Wood at City University London plotted more than 1.5 million pictures taken by 45,000 users on Flickr, the popular photo-sharing site. Like camera flashes in a dark arena, these lines and clusters expose patterns of human activity. Purple dots indicate photographs taken in low light conditions, such as inside a museum or at night; yellow indicates images made in the bright light of day, often in parks and squares or along the Thames, Regent's Canal and The Serpentine. Turn the page to zoom in on Westminster.

Flickr photographs by luminance
January 2008 – June 2013

Day   Outdoor

Night   Indoor

SOURCE: FLICKR

Portobello
Road Market

Paddington
Station

Marble
Arch

NOTTING HILL

*Kensington
Gardens*

Hyde Park

*Round
Pond*

The Serpentine

0 _____ 500 m

Thousands of images outline
The Serpentine in yellow
while the museums of South
Kensington create purple
clusters as visitors snap pics
inside them. The Palace of
Westminster and London
Eye inspire shots along the
Thames. Further east on
South Bank, people turn
their lenses towards the
dome of St Paul's and Tate
Modern's Turbine Hall.

Royal
Albert Hall

Harrods

Science
Museum

Victoria and
Albert Museum

Natural History
Museum

SOURCE: FLICKR; ALEXANDER KACHKAEV AND JO WOOD, CITY UNIVERSITY LONDON

Okapi **3**

Golden-headed lion tamarin **4**

Pygmy hippo **2**

Rodrigues flying fox **27**

Southern tamandua **2**

Axolotl **13**

Gaboon caecilian **12**

Mastigure **4**

McCord's snake-necked turtle **7**

Mountain chicken frog **37**

Komodo dragon **2**

Number of each species in the 2014 inventory

A True Zoo

The Zoological Society of London (ZSL) counts its creatures, big and small.

ZSL London Zoo's Sumatran tigers, Jae Jae and Melati, made headlines in February 2014 when Melati gave birth to three cubs: Budi, Nakal and Cinta. More tigers means more visitors. Still, the world's oldest research zoo hopes people will find wonder in all 758 of its species. Here we celebrate some lesser-known creatures tallied during the zoo's annual inventory. Whilst keepers monitor animal counts daily,

ZSL London Zoo animal inventory 2014

209 reptiles *(63 species)*

571 mammals   584 birds   684 amphibians   4,903 fish

9,918 invertebrates

59 species   113 species   24 species   276 species

223 species

Red-crested turaco 5

Malayan black hornbill 3

Leaf insect 21

Brittlestar 158

Jaraqui 8

Lobetoothed piranha 15

Tawny frogmouth 7

Partula snail 2,158

Goliath bird-eating tarantula 1

Cichlid 28
Haplotaxodon trifasciatus

Western hercules beetle 1

Emerald cockroach wasp 9

Northern helmeted curassow 2

Hamerkop 2

Colored tuxedo urchin 6

Royal twig catfish 9

Australian lungfish 3

the zoo's licence requires them to log an official 'stocktake' into the International Species Information System's global database of 374,000 living animals. This allows ZSL to collaborate with other zoos and governments on breeding programmes for endangered species of all sizes. Thanks to these efforts, three species of Partula snails are back in the trees of Tahiti for the first time since the 1970s.

Nearly 60% of the zoo's animals do not have a backbone. That figure would be much higher if ZSL didn't count its thousands of honeybees and leaf-cutter ants as single colonies.

TOTAL
16,869 animals
758 species

SOURCE: ZOOLOGICAL SOCIETY OF LONDON. SKETCHES: OLIVER UBERTI

All the Tate's Treasures

Wall space isn't an issue online.

Art lovers rejoice. The Tate art galleries have put all 70,000 works in their collection of British art and international modern and contemporary art online in a database searchable by artist, decade, subject, even emotion. Here we show the 106 artists with at least fifty works in the collection.

No one comes close to J. M. W. Turner, the great painter and Londoner who bequeathed the contents of his studio to the nation in 1851. His bequest includes 280 sketchbooks from his travels and 30,000 preparatory drawings and watercolours like this one. The two large oils he made of this subject hang in museums in Cleveland and Philadelphia, USA. But those are also viewable on the Tate's website.

Artists with 50 or more works in the Tate collection
June 2014

Painter, printmaker
Sculptor
Photographer

YEAR OF BIRTH ▸

Francis Barlow **109**

Joseph Highmore **79**

Richard Wilson **66**

Alexander Cozens **237**

Susanna Duncombe **76**

Thomas Gainsborough **158**

Sir Nathaniel Dance-Holland **169**

Philip James de Loutherbourg **91**

Heneage Finch **50**

Sir George Beaumont **62**

John Flaxman **287**

Thomas Stothard **215**

William Blake **180**

Prince Hoare **64**

Joshua Cristall **85**

William Daniell **612**

Francois Louis Francia **63**

Thomas Girtin **94**

John Constable

1650   1700   1750

J. M. W. Turner (1775–1851)

39,389 works

◀ The Burning of the Houses of Parliament
1834–5
Watercolour and gouache on paper

John Scarlett Davis — 104
Elizabeth Rigby — 60
William James Muller — 82
Charles Martin — 68
Charles Keene — 54
Dante Gabriel Rossetti — 55
Sir John Everett Millais — 64
Sir Edward Burne-Jones — 138

Barnett Freedman — 54
John Piper — 183
Ceri Richards — 89
Graham Sutherland — 55
Victor Pasmore — 135
Cecil Collins — 75
Francis Bacon — 50
Julian Trevelyan — 105

Robert Motherwell — 74
Sir Terry Frost — 51
Sir Sidney Nolan — 135
Leon Ferrari — 199
Patrick Heron — 92
Joseph Beuys — 578

Richard Hamilton — 138
Diane Arbus — 69
Leon Kossoff — 116
Andy Warhol — 272
Joe Tilson — 152

Sol LeWitt — 94
Harold Cohen — 52
Keith Arnatt — 133
Robyn Denny — 85
Dieter Roth — 60
Richard Smith — 96
Frank Auerbach — 76

Christopher Le Brun — 65

R. B. Kitaj — 179
Gordon House — 110
Howard Hodgkin — 68
Ian Tyson — 93
Ivor Abrahams — 108
Patrick Caulfield — 124
Gerd Winner — 122
Martin Kippenberger — 109

Frank Stella — 66
Tom Phillips — 274
David Hockney — 111
Georg Baselitz — 68
Brice Marden — 64
Damien Hirst — 54

Walter Sickert — 50
Ben Nicholson — 80
William Roberts — 142

Sir Stanley Spencer — 63

Per Kirkeby — 56
John Walker — 135
Colin Self — 76
Robert Mapplethorpe — 75
Steven Sorman — 60
Akram Zaatari — 119

Henry Moore — 623

Terry Winters — 76
Wolfgang Tillmans — 63

249
John Varley — 102
John Sell Cotman — 92
William Henry Hunt — 81

Sir Augustus Callcott — 87
David Cox — 60
George Jones — 1,046
John Linnell — 72

55
Sir David Wilkie — 60
Clarkson Fred Stanfield — 84

Lady Wharncliffe

Julio Gonzalez — 56
Eric Gill — 128
Naum Gabo — 132

Jacques Lipchitz — 62
Henri Gaudier-Brzeska — 60

Dame Barbara Hepworth — 123
William Turnbull — 69
Sir Eduardo Paolozzi — 385

Ian Hamilton Finlay — 164
Dame Elisabeth Frink — 125
Kim Lim — 59
Allen Jones — 59

Barry Flanagan — 162

Thomas Schutte — 156

1800 **1850** **1900** **1950**

2 1 3

HEIGHT (metres)

❶ High Roller
Las Vegas, United States – 2014
HEIGHT 168 metres   **CAPACITY** 1,120 (*28 cabins* x 40 *seats*)
DURATION 30 minutes

❷ Singapore Flyer
Singapore – 2008
HEIGHT 165 m   **CAPACITY** 784 (28x28)
DURATION 37 minutes

❸ Star of Nanchang
Nanchang, China – 2006
HEIGHT 160 m   **CAPACITY** 480 (60x8)
DURATION 30 minutes

❹ London Eye
London, UK– 1999
HEIGHT 135 m   **CAPACITY** 800 (32x25)
DURATION 30 minutes

❺ Suzhou Ferris Wheel
Suzhou, China – 2009
HEIGHT 120 m   **CAPACITY** 300 (60x5)
DURATION 20 minutes

❿ Diamond and Flower Wheel
Tokyo, Japan – 2001
HEIGHT 117 m   **CAPACITY** 408 (68x6)
DURATION 17 minutes

❾ Zhengzhou Ferris Wheel
Zhengzhou, China – 2003
HEIGHT 120 m   **CAPACITY** 324 (54x6)
DURATION 30 minutes

❽ Changsha Ferris Wheel
Changsha, China – 2004
HEIGHT 120 m   **CAPACITY** 480 (60x8)
DURATION 20 minutes

❼ Tianjin Eye
Tianjin, China – 2008
HEIGHT 120 m   **CAPACITY** 384 (48x8)
DURATION 30 minutes

❻ The Melbourne Star
Melbourne, Australia – 2008
HEIGHT 120 m   **CAPACITY** 420 (21x20)
DURATION 30 minutes

⓫ Sun Wheel
Da Nang, Vietnam – 2014
HEIGHT 115 m   **CAPACITY** 384 (64x6)
DURATION 15 minutes

⓬ Star of Lake Tai
Lake Tai, China – 2008
HEIGHT 115 m   **CAPACITY** 384 (64x6)
DURATION 18 minutes

⓭ Daikanransha at Palette Town
Odaiba, Japan – 1999
HEIGHT 115 m   **CAPACITY** 384 (64x6)
DURATION 16 minutes

⓮ Cosmo Clock 21
Yokohama, Japan - 1999
HEIGHT 113 m   **CAPACITY** 480 (60x8)
DURATION 15 minutes

⓯ Tempozan Ferris Wheel
Osaka, Japan – 1997
HEIGHT 112 m   **CAPACITY** 480 (60x8)
DURATION 15 minutes

㉚ Wiener Riesenrad
Vienna, Austria – 1897
HEIGHT 65 m   **CAPACITY** 180 (15x12)
DURATION 10 minutes

㉙ Texas Star
Dallas, US – 1985
HEIGHT 65 m   **CAPACITY** 264 (44x6)
DURATION 12 minutes

㉘ Miramar Ferris Wheel
Taipei, Taiwan – 2002
HEIGHT 70 m   **CAPACITY** 288 (48x6)
DURATION 17 minutes

㉗ Polaris Tower
Daejon, South Korea – 1993
HEIGHT 72 m   **CAPACITY** 288 (36x8)
DURATION no data

㉖ Moscow-850
Moscow, Russia – 1997
HEIGHT 73 m   **CAPACITY** 320 (40x8)
DURATION 7 minutes

Following the Leader

Cities around the world have been eyeing up the London Eye.

When the London Eye opened in 2000, it was the tallest observation wheel in the world. Over the course of a 30-minute ride, the thirty-two cars lift passengers to a height of 135 metres for unprecedented views of Westminster and beyond. The wheel became an instant symbol of prosperity. Every major world city wanted one. The Eye was eventually topped by the Star of Nanchang in 2006 and then the Singapore Flyer in 2008. Plans for at least five larger wheels in Beijing, Berlin, Dubai, Jeddah and Orlando were scrapped, leaving London's in the top three until the 168-metre High Roller opened in Las Vegas in March 2014.

HEIGHT (m)

16 Harbin Ferris Wheel
Harbin, China – 2003
HEIGHT 110 m   CAPACITY 378 (63x6)
DURATION 20 minutes

17 Shanghai Ferris Wheel
Shanghai, China – 2003
HEIGHT 108 m   CAPACITY 378 (63x6)
DURATION 25 minutes

18 Space Eye
Kitakyushu, Japan – 1990
HEIGHT 100 m   CAPACITY 264 (44x6)
DURATION no data

19 Aurora Wheel
Kuwana, Japan
HEIGHT 90 m   CAPACITY 480 (60x8)
DURATION no data

20 Eurowheel
Ravenna, Italy – 1999
HEIGHT 90 m   CAPACITY 400 (50x8)
DURATION 11 minutes

25 HEP Five
Osaka, Japan – 1998
HEIGHT 75 m   CAPACITY 208 (52x4)
DURATION 15 minutes

24 Mashhad Ferris Wheel
Mashhad, Iran – 2005
HEIGHT 80 m   CAPACITY 336 (56x6)
DURATION no data

23 Tbilisi Ferris Wheel
Tbilisi, Geogia – 2010
HEIGHT 80 m   CAPACITY 264 (44x6)
DURATION 15 minutes

22 Sochi Ferris Wheel
Sochi, Russia – 2012
HEIGHT 80 m   CAPACITY 112 (28x4)
DURATION 10 minutes

21 Sky Wheel
Gukeng, Taiwan – 1990
HEIGHT 88 m   CAPACITY 400 (50x8)
DURATION 15 minutes

GRAPHIC: FRANCESCO FRANCHI, ALESSANDRO GIBERTI, *IL SOLE 24 ORE*. ILLUSTRATIONS: LAURA CATTANEO. ADDITIONAL SOURCE: OBSERVATION WHEEL DIRECTORY

NEW YORK
6–13 February

LONDON
14–18 February

Fashion Cycles

The London fog appears to be lifting.

The world's top designers are preparing for another blustery winter. Warmth and comfort are in. Oversized parkas, turtlenecks, quilting, shaggy furs, layers and leopard prints dominated the runways during international fashion month in February 2014. Style and fit weren't the only effects of the cold. The world's colour palette shifted, too. EDITD, a London-based fashion analytics firm, extracted colour data from photographs of every garment shown at each of the four

MILAN
18–23 February

PARIS
25 February – 5 March

fashion weeks in New York, London, Milan and Paris to create the wheels above. In addition to glacial blues, forest greens and the drinkable tones of red wines, the Autumn-Winter 2014 palette features unseasonably vivid colours to brighten moods on dreary days. Of the four fashion capitals, London can look forward to the least muted palette. Nearly a third of the looks cleared away the dreary greys in favour of sunshine hues.

Percentage of garments shown during each international fashion week by colour
Autumn-Winter 2014

New York and Paris bookended the month with support for the pastels that were popular in the spring lines. Milan elected for the most muted palette, opting for more shades of coffee, oatmeal and granite than the other cities.

They Came,
They Saw,
They Spent

In terms of spending per visitor, Arab tourists reign.

If the 2012 Olympics were supposed to be an elaborate marketing campaign for the capital, it worked. 16.8 million overseas visitors came to London in 2013, the highest recorded total since 1961. Continuing a 43.5% rise in international visits since 2003, the banner year unseated Paris (16.6m) as Europe's most visited city. Backpackers on a shoestring these were not. Altogether, they dropped £11 billion.

   The Olympics can't claim all the credit though. For the past five years, Ramadan – the Muslim month of fasting – has coincided with the heat of summer. Before it begins, millionaires from Gulf Arab states like Saudi Arabia have been escaping to London for a few weeks. While American tourists spent the most as a country, as we show to the right, they can't compete with Saudis in terms of spending per visitor. The average American spends £800 on a trip to London. The average Saudi will spend over triple that. Many retailers are now hiring Arabic-speaking staff to welcome them.

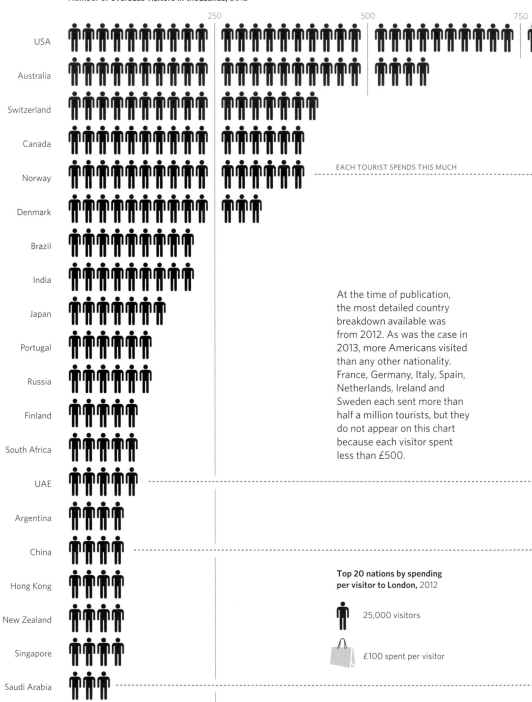

Number of overseas visitors in thousands, 2012

USA · Australia · Switzerland · Canada · Norway · Denmark · Brazil · India · Japan · Portugal · Russia · Finland · South Africa · UAE · Argentina · China · Hong Kong · New Zealand · Singapore · Saudi Arabia

EACH TOURIST SPENDS THIS MUCH

At the time of publication, the most detailed country breakdown available was from 2012. As was the case in 2013, more Americans visited than any other nationality. France, Germany, Italy, Spain, Netherlands, Ireland and Sweden each sent more than half a million tourists, but they do not appear on this chart because each visitor spent less than £500.

Top 20 nations by spending per visitor to London, 2012

25,000 visitors

£100 spent per visitor

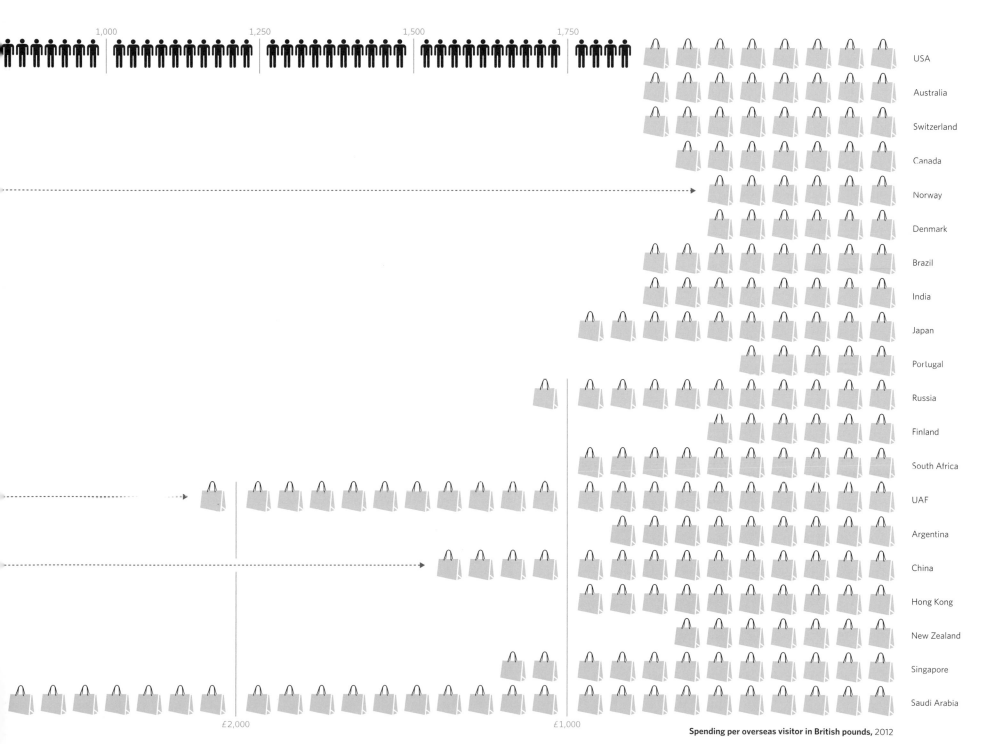

1,000   1,250   1,500   1,750

USA
Australia
Switzerland
Canada
Norway
Denmark
Brazil
India
Japan
Portugal
Russia
Finland
South Africa
UAF
Argentina
China
Hong Kong
New Zealand
Singapore
Saudi Arabia

£2,000   £1,000

Spending per overseas visitor in British pounds, 2012

Shop Window

London's supermarkets fragment the city.

In this graphic, we drew a line halfway between every major super-market or convenience store and its next nearest to show how far Londoners have to travel for their closest shop. What emerges is a stained-glass window of consumer choice.

Though people don't always use their closest store, they won't go too far out of their way to visit a competitor. This distance varies with transport mode. Relatively few people have cars in more central areas. They shop locally and often to avoid carrying too much. Stores in outer boroughs tend to be bigger and offer large car parks to their custom-ers, who will travel a little further for a big 'weekly' shop.

Supermarkets, April 2014

- Waitrose
- Tesco
- Sainsbury's
- Morrisons
- Asda
- Iceland
- Co-Op
- Lidl
- Aldi
- ● Supermarket

We all forget the milk from time to time, so big brands like Sainsbury's (orange) and Tesco (blue) have been sticking smaller convenience stores near Tube and train stations to attract commuters on their way home. Waitrose (green) is popular with the wealthy set; Aldi (light blue) and Lidl (yellow) can be found in less affluent areas.

SOURCES: FOOD STANDARDS AGENCY; OSM

HARINGEY

WALTHAM FOREST

CAMDEN

HACKNEY

BRENT

ISLINGTON

NEWHAM

TOWER HAMLETS

CITY

KENSINGTON & CHELSEA

River Thames

WESTMINSTER

HAMMERSMITH & FULHAM

SOUTHWARK

GREENWICH

LAMBETH

LEWISHAM

WANDSWORTH

0   1 km

Who Says Print is Dead?

Londoners love newspapers.

Despite the growing prevalence of digital news, millions of pages of newsprint still appear in London every morning. Veteran papers like the *Guardian*, *The Times* and the *Daily Telegraph* maintain loyal readerships, but more Londoners get their news from free dailies than any other paper. They read the *METRO* on their morning commutes and the *London Evening Standard* on their rides home. In fact, so many *METRO* papers are delivered each day in the capital that if stacked they would tower 1,915 metres above the city – more than the height of six Shards!

HEIGHT
(metres)

1,500 ——

1,000 ——

1,915 m
London only

3,390 m
National
circulation

2,450 m

1,729 m

1,717 m

6
Shards

5
Shards

4
Shards

WHAT WE LIKE

National daily circulation, March 2014

8,000 metres
25 Shards

7,748 m — Sun

4,451 — Daily Mail

3,390 — METRO

ENLARGED
BELOW

4,000

6 Shards

Daily Telegraph
The Times
Evening Standard
Financial Times
Guardian
Independent

Tower heights multiply circulation by the approximate thickness of each paper.

3 Shards

2 Shards

310 metres

820 m

520 m

100 metres

500

Independent	Guardian	Financial Times	London Evening Standard	The Times	Daily Telegraph	METRO	The Shard
66,500 papers	208,000	234,000	687,000	384,000	545,000	766,000	

SOURCE: WIKIPEDIA

2 2 3

The Buzz About Town

The capital's premier blog keeps Londoners in the know.

Since 2004, *Londonist* – originally titled *The Big Smoker* – has covered both the serious and slightly quirkier sides to the capital. Contributors report on breaking news as well as how to queue for the Wimbledon Championships, 'weird facts you probably didn't know' and the ever-popular 'Free & Cheap' things to do in the capital. They 'tag' each post with searchable terms like 'Boris Johnson' or 'frugal fun'. Below, we took every tag used more than fifteen times between 2008 and 2013 and grouped them by theme. We then charted the number of times they were used to see what London was talking about each month. Christmas chatter increased each year, whilst the Olympics quickly became old news.

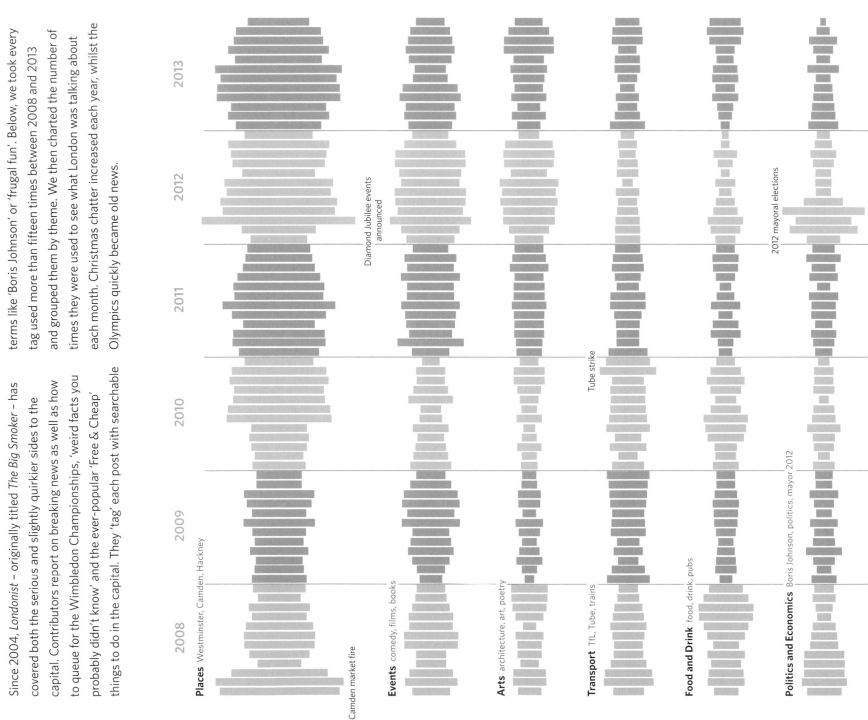

2008   2009   2010   2011   2012   2013

Places Westminster, Camden, Hackney

Camden market fire

Events comedy, films, books

Diamond Jubilee events announced

Arts architecture, art, poetry

Transport TfL, Tube, trains

Tube strike

Food and Drink food, drink, pubs

Politics and Economics Boris Johnson, politics, mayor 2012

2012 mayoral elections

SOURCE: LONDONIST.COM

Theatre and Cinema cinema, Sadlers Wells, National Theatre

London film festival

Things to Do Things To Do, whats on, stuff to do

Museums exhibition, Museums & Galleries, Tate Modern

Olympics Olympics, 2012, London 2012

London 2012

Beijing 2008

Photography Flickr, Photo of the Day, seasonal photo

Sport sport, cycling, football

Free Free & Cheap, cheap, frugal fun

Crime and Terrorism crime, police, Metropolitan Police

Riots

Science science, weekly geek listings, geek

Seasonal Christmas, santa's lap, Christmas 2013

Christmas

Launch of hand-drawn maps competition

Maps maps, hand-drawn maps of London

Royalty royal wedding, Queen, Prince George

Royal Wedding

Queen's Diamond Jubilee

WHAT WE LIKE

J F M A M J J A S O N D J F M A M J J A S O N D J F M A M J J A S O N D

Looking for Love

Who wants who online.

Searching for a soulmate can feel like fumbling around in a dark room: you can only see what's in the beam of your torch. Online dating sites like *lovestruck.com* offer a wider beam. Yet most users choose to narrow theirs to a desired age range spanning around fourteen years. The question then becomes not how wide is the beam but in what direction is it pointing? Younger or older?

On the right we show the average desired age ranges of Londoners of four sexual orientations at five different ages: 22, 32, 42, 52 and 62. Brighter areas show the most desired ages where multiple searchlights overlap. In general, twenty-two-year-olds tend to have the narrowest search, with the exception of gay men who were open to dating men more than ten years older. As straight men get older they continue to look for increasingly younger partners, but (surprise!) so do straight women. Fifty-two-year-old gay men cast the widest searches; by 62 though, they begin to search among their peers. Older gay women also cast a wide net, but overall, age appears less important to them; sixty-two-year-old gay women were the only demographic in our sample searching for companions in their seventies.

Average desired age ranges of approved Lovestruck profiles in London, April 2014

In 2012, the Office for National Statistics asked 180,000 respondents to its Integrated Household Survey about their sexual identity at the time. 2.5% of Londoners answered gay, lesbian or bisexual adult, the highest percentage in the UK. There aren't many same-sex searches on Lovestruck because other dating services dominate those markets.

2,700

MEN *seeking* **MEN**

54,000

MEN *seeking* WOMEN

70,000

WOMEN *seeking* **MEN**

1,200

WOMEN *seeking* WOMEN

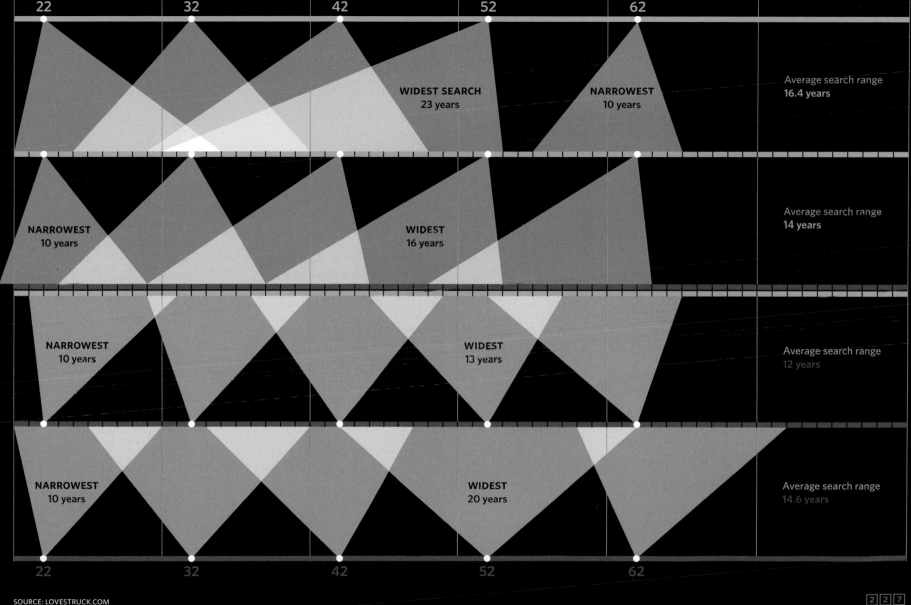

22　32　42　52　62

WIDEST SEARCH
23 years

NARROWEST
10 years

Average search range
16.4 years

NARROWEST
10 years

WIDEST
16 years

Average search range
14 years

NARROWEST
10 years

WIDEST
13 years

Average search range
12 years

NARROWEST
10 years

WIDEST
20 years

Average search range
14.6 years

22　32　42　52　62

Happy Times

Cheer increases as the day progresses.

In 2010, George MacKerron, now a lecturer at the University of Sussex, set out to gauge the nation's happiness. His idea was simple: create an iPhone app that 'pings' people a few times a day to ask how happy they are and what they are doing at the time. He thought he would be lucky if a thousand people signed up. One year later, more than 40,000 people had shared several million answers to his questions, making 'Mappiness' one of the largest ever surveys of subjective well-being.

Londoners make up about twenty per cent of the app's user base. Their responses are shown here. From left to right the time of day runs from 8 a.m. to 10 p.m.; from top to bottom the day of the year runs from 1 September 2010 to 31 August 2011. The stripe pattern highlights the city's mood swings. Weekends and holidays make people happy (yellow); weekday mornings find them feeling blue.

London's happiness, September 2010 – September 2011

UNHAPPY ▬▬▬▬▬▬▬▬▬▬▬▬ HAPPY

A swathe of yellow in late April shows Londoners enjoying a national holiday for the Royal Wedding between Prince William and the then Kate Middleton.

Large splashes of yellow appear in late December and mid-April during the Christmas and Easter breaks. Note the very happy period late on New Year's Eve.

1 p.m. 2 p.m. 3 p.m. 4 p.m. 5 p.m. 6 p.m. 7 p.m. 8 p.m. 9 p.m.

September
October
November
December
January
February
March
April
May
June
July
August

CHRISTMAS DAY

NEW YEAR'S EVE

EASTER

Further Reading

ON LONDON

One of the joys of creating *London: The Information Capital* has been getting to know the city better through its great books and websites. These have provided us with inspiration and much needed context to the graphics we have created.

London: The Biography by Peter Ackroyd (2001) offers the most in depth introduction to the past life and times of the city and augments the visual introductions offered by *London: The Illustrated History* (Cathy Ross and John Clark, 2008) and the excellent *Times History of London* (Hugh Clout, 1999). Map addicts will thoroughly enjoy *London: A History in Maps* (Peter Barber, 2012) and the wealth of historic maps in the British Library's Crace Collection online gallery (*www.bl.uk/onlinegallery/onlineex/crace*). The Mapping London blog (*mappinglondon.co.uk*) regularly posts more up to date cartographic representations of the capital as does Londonist (*londonist com*).

To get to know Londoners past and present, we would recommend Steven Johnson's *The Ghost Map* (2006) that details how John Snow took on cholera, and the BBC TV series and associated book entitled *The Secret History of Our Streets* (2012) that compares Charles Booth's London with the contemporary city. Craig Taylor's *Londoners* (2011) shares the personal stories of those who have made the city their home and reminds us that behind every data point is a person.

Finally, the ultimate reference book for London is *The London Encyclopaedia* (Ben Weinreb, Christopher Hibbert, Julia Keay, John Keay. 3rd Edition, 2010). Hours could be spent jumping from one entry to another and the sheer volume of information it contains is worthy of a graphic by itself.

If you have been inspired to create your own graphics, the London Datastore (*data.london.gov.uk*) is the best place to start for any data you might need.

ON INFORMATION GRAPHICS & DESIGN

There are many great instructional books on information graphics. To save yourself time and shelf space, start with *Cartographies of Time* (Daniel Rosenberg and Anthony Grafton, 2010), *The Functional Art: An Introduction to Information Graphics and Visualization* (Alberto Cairo, 2013) or *Visualize This: The FlowingData Guide to Visualization, Design and Statistics* (Nathan Yau, 2011).

Any discussion about the process of making maps and graphics must include the writings of Edward Tufte. Our 'Causes of Death' graphic pays homage to his 'sparklines', while the principles outlined in his classic trio – *Envisioning Information* (1990), *Visual Explanations* (1997) and *The Visual Display of Quantitative Information* (2001) – guided our thinking throughout the book.

For designers in search of the perfect typeface for their next project, we highly recommend *The Anatomy of Type: A Graphic Guide to 100 Typefaces* (Stephen Coles, 2012). If you are looking for inspiration, new graphic forms or best practices, pick up the latest copy of the *Guardian, National Geographic* or *The New York Times*. The data teams at those three publications continually raise the bar for what we can communicate through visuals.

ON MAPS

Infinite Perspectives: Two Thousand Years of Three-Dimensional Mapmaking (1999) shows how maps can literally jump off the page. *How to Lie with Maps* by Mark Monmonier (1996) is a classic amongst cartographers seeking to produce maps that don't mislead, and Denis Wood's *Rethinking the Power of Maps* (2010) is a reminder that maps can be extremely influential in the right (or wrong) hands.

① Royal Geographical Society
② Victoria & Albert Museum
③ Daunt Books
④⑤⑦ Grant Museum of Zoology / UCL / Church of Christ the King
⑤ UCL
⑥ King's Cross St Pancras
⑦ Church of Christ the King
⑧ Waterstones
⑨ The Building Centre
⑩ British Museum
⑪
⑫ Stanfords
⑬
⑭ South Bank
⑮ Ye Olde Cheshire Cheese
⑯ Borough Market
⑰ Vagabond N7
⑱ Zuccino Coffee
⑲ Hoxton Street Monster Supplies
⑳ Brick Lane

Bookstores & coffee shops
July 2014

📖 Independent bookstore
☕ Coffee shop
Ⓣ Tube, DLR or Overground station

0 |————————————| 1 km

Books, Coffee, etc.

When Oliver came to London, I drew him a few maps to find his way around.

We decided to do the same for you. Here are a few spots to fuel your mind.

1 Royal Geographical Society
The heart of geography in the UK hosts Monday night lectures by explorers and academics alike as well as excellent, and often map-based, exhibitions during the year.

2 Victoria and Albert Museum
Get lost among 2.4 million objects spanning art, design, fashion and architecture. Then find yourself in the museum's Victorian café.

3 Daunt Books Marylebone
An Edwardian bookshop focusing on non-fiction and literature.

4 Grant Museum of Zoology
Home to a jar of moles, skeletons and an extensive collection of bisected animal heads, it's not for the faint-hearted!

5 University College London
Jeremy Bentham's dressed skeleton and wax head (with his real hair) is on display. To this day, 'Bentham' attends the occasional UCL Board meeting.

6 John Betjeman Statue
St Pancras station offers the grandest gateway into London. Betjeman helped to preserve it and is rewarded with its best view.

7 Church of Christ the King
Oliver's parents were married there in 1970 when it was the church for London's universities.

8 Waterstones Gower Street
Housed in Gower Street's most elaborate building, this bookshop has an excellent London section alongside a huge collection of second-hand books and remainders.

9 The Building Centre
Head here to view a giant 3D model of central London.

10 British Museum
Did you know it has a Prints and Drawings collection with rare linocuts by Picasso?

11 John Snow Pub
Epidemiologists, historians and geographers make pilgrimages to this pub across the street from the infamous pump its namesake identified (see pp. 30–31).

12 Stanfords Bookshop
The world's biggest travel bookshop was our first port of call for books and maps about the capital.

13 Waterloo Bridge
The view is unparalleled.

14 South Bank
This cultural hub makes for a nice evening stroll from the London Eye to Tower Bridge.

15 Ye Olde Cheshire Cheese Pub
Dickens frequented this pub off Fleet Steet and sent characters there to dine in *A Tale of Two Cities*.

16 Borough Market
Start a Saturday morning sampling fruits, cheeses, bread and coffee – if you can stand the crowds.

17 Vagabond No. 7
When you've been caught in a downpour, the espresso and eggs here will warm you up.

18 Zuccino Coffee
Along Camden passage in Angel, its small garden is the place to sip a flat white on sunnier days.

19 Hoxton Street Monster Supplies
Running low on heebie-jeebies? Stop by this shop on Hoxton Street. All purchases support the Ministry of Stories (see pp. 198–9).

20 Brick Lane
Curry houses. Enough said.

21 Museum of London Docklands
The best place to connect with London's nautical past and learn how the East End is changing.

22 Over the O$_2$
With the Thames on three sides and Canary Wharf opposite, the roof of the O$_2$ Arena offers a stunning panorama of London.

23 Blackheath Point
You can take in a dramatic sunset from this Protected Vista (see pp. 68–73) without the crowds of Primrose Hill or Greenwich Park.

SOURCES: BOOKSELLERS ASSOCIATION; LONDON COFFEE GUIDE; OSM

Notes

Open data from the Office for National Statistics (ONS), Ordnance Survey (OS), and OpenStreetMap (OSM) have been essential to this book. We abbreviated their credits on graphics; we include it in full here:

ONS: Office for National Statistics licensed under the Open Government Licence v.2.0.

OS: Contains Ordnance Survey data © Crown copyright and database right 2014

OSM: © OpenStreetMap contributors CC BY-SA

Any additional data sources are credited as fully as possible at the bottom of each graphic or in their associated text.

All the URLs listed below were live in August 2014.

_____

INTRODUCTION *(pp. 20-33)*

For more on Phyllis Pearsall and the creation of the first *A to Z*, see: *designmuseum.org/design/phyllis-pearsall*

For more on Henry Beck's Tube map – and many others – see Mark Ovenden's *Metro Maps of the World* (London: Capital Transport Publishing, 2nd Ed. 2005).

The Open Data Rankings come from the *2013 Open Data Barometer*: *www.opendataresearch.org/dl/odb2013/Open-Data-Barometer-2013-Global-Report.pdf*

The conversation between Gordon Brown and Sir Tim Berners-Lee is quoted from the *Guardian*: *www.theguardian.com/commentisfree/2010/nov/06/google-da-vid-cameron-copyright*

Francis Maude, Minister for the Cabinet Office, frequently talks about the British Government's commitment to open data: *www.gov.uk/government/speeches/francis-maude-speech-on-transparency.* This follows the government white paper entitled *Open Data: Unleashing the Potential: data.gov.uk/sites/default/files/Open_data_White_Paper.pdf*

The UK's Open Government License is detailed here: *www.nationalarchives.gov.uk/doc/open-government-licence*

More on the Information Commissioner's Office and Freedom of Information Requests appears here: *ico.org.uk/for_organisations/freedom_of_information/guide*

More on the Ordnance Survey can be found here: *www.ordnancesurvey.co.uk/about/overview/activities.html* and a history of the census in England and Wales can be found on the ONS's website: *www.ons.gov.uk/ons/guide-method/census/2011/how-our-census-works/about-censuses/census-history/index.html*

For additional research on Booth's work, see the London School of Economics's online archive: *booth.lse.ac.uk*

The Science Museum has a brief biography of William Farr: *www.sciencemuseum.org.uk/broughttolife/people/williamfarr.aspx*

The Ghost Map (Steven Johnson, London: Penguin, 2006) details the work of John Snow.

WHERE WE ARE

Contours of the City (36-7)

The origin of London at the lowest convenient crossing point of the Thames is outlined on p. 494 of *The London Encyclopedia* (Weinreb, Hibbert, Keay, Keay. London: Macmillan, 2008).

We checked our historic rivers against the *Times History of London* (Hugh Clout, 1999) and the *Atlas of London* (Emrys Jones and Daniel Sinclair, 1968).

What we talk about when we talk about London (38-9)

Peter Ackroyd's full quote from p. 779 of *London: The Biography* (London: Vintage, 2001) reads: 'London goes beyond any boundary or convention. It contains every wish or word ever spoken, every action or gesture ever made, every harsh or noble statement ever expressed. It is illimitable. It is Infinite London.'

The origins of Ealing, Greenwich and Arsenal come from their entries in *The London Encyclopedia* (Weinreb, Hibbert, Keay, Keay. London: Macmillan, 2008)

Hub for the World (40-41)

Heathrow Airport has its full history outlined here: *en.wikipedia.org/wiki/History_of_London_Heathrow_Airport*

Heathrow was ranked first in terms of international passenger traffic in 2013 by Airport Councils International: *en.wikipedia.org/wiki/World's_busiest_airports_by_international_passenger_traffic*

From Home to Work (42-3)

The commuting time data are taken from the ONS's *Commuting to Work* report from 2 June 2011: *www.ons.gov.uk/ons/dcp171776_227904.pdf*

The estimate for London's wider metropolitan area was taken from EPSON, but there are others. See here: *en.wikipedia.org/wiki/List_of_metropolitan_areas_in_Europe*

Hot Spots (46-7)

For more on the urban heat island effect, see *National Geographic's* online entry: *education.nationalgeographic.co.uk/education/encyclopedia/urban-heat-island*

Seeking Shade (48-9)

For more on London's trees, see *The Mayor's Street Tree Programme Final Evaluation Report* published in 2012 by the Mayor of London: *www.london.gov.uk/sites/default/files/archives/mstp_evaluation_winter_2012.pdf*

The Urban Wild (50-51)

The Daniel Raven-Ellison quote was taken from a press release promoting the start of the Greater London National Park campaign. For more details: *www.greaterlondonnationalpark.org.uk*

Holding Back the Tide (52-3)

London's Victorian embankments were built by Sir Joseph Bazalgette to house sewers taking effluent downstream out of the city. See p. 272 of *The London Encyclopedia* (Weinreb, Hibbert, Keay, Keay. London: Macmillan, 2008) for more information.

The BBC has a good article on the 1928 flood of London: *www.bbc.co.uk/news/magazine-26153241* and the GLA has details from the 1953 flood: *www.london.gov.uk/mayor-assembly/mayor/london-resilience/london-prepared-blog/2013/01/remembering-the-1953-floods*

For more on how the Thames Barrier works and its use at the start of 2014, see: *www.gov.uk/the-thames-barrier*

The London Assembly Environment Committee published a report in April 2014 entitled *Flood Risks In London: www.london.gov.uk/sites/default/files/14-04-07-Flood%20risk%20slide%20pack%20-%20FINAL_0.pdf*

What Lies Beneath (56-7)

To produce our text and drawings, Crossrail gave us access to their image library and Archaeological Sites summary, but there's plenty of good info available to the public at *www.crossrail.co.uk*

Back From the Blitz (62-3)

The BBC has a detailed account of the Blitz and its death toll: *www.bbc.co.uk/history/events/germany_bombs_london*

(Un)Affordable Flats (66-7)

The 'more billionaires than any other city' statement is drawn from the *Sunday Times* Rich List reported here: *www.channel4.com/news/london-sunday-times-super-rich-list-billionaires*

For more on the dynamics of people buying or renting their homes, see here: *www.ons.gov.uk/ons/rel/census/2011-census-analysis/a-century-of-home-ownership-and-renting-in-england-and-wales/short-story-on-housing.html*

We based our mortgage affordability on this advice: *www.which.co.uk/money/mortgages-and-property/guides/mortgage-deposit-explained/how-much-deposit-do-i-need-for-a-mortgage*

Our median income calculation is based on 2013 figures from the ONS quoted here: *www.ons.gov.uk/ons/dcp171778_335027.pdf*

13 Views Worth Protecting (68-73)

Each protected vista is detailed in the London View Management Framework published by the GLA in 2012: *legacy.london.gov.uk/ mayor/strategies/sds/docs/spg- views-final-all.pdf*

As of Spring 2014, 230 sky-scrapers were planned for London according to the *London's Growing Up!* report by New London Architects. *www.newlondonarchitecture. org/dls/TB_B1.pdf*

WHO WE ARE

Why it's worth knowing who we are (78-9)

The quote from the Royal Statistical Society is taken from its response to the consultation on the census and the future provision of population statistics in England and Wales, published December 2013: *www.rss.org. uk/uploadedfiles/userfiles/files/ RSS%20Beyond%202011%20con sultation%20response%20Decem- ber%202013.pdf*

The threat of cancelling the 2011 Census was detailed in a letter to the Chair of the UK Statistics Authority. His response can be viewed here: *statisticsauthority. gov.uk/reports---correspondence/ correspondence/letter-from-sir-mi- chael-scholar-to-francis-maude-mp- --20-may-2010.pdf*

In July 2014, the UK govern-ment announced there would be a census in 2021. They also said, 'It is the government's ambition

that beyond 2021 the decennial census would not be undertaken. Instead, more regular and timely administrative data would be used to produce statistics.' *www.ft.com/ cms/s/0/4313fd34-1586-11e4- 9e18-00144feabdc0.html#axzz- 38kdBejkX*

Similarities Attract (80-81)

For more on the London Output Area Classification, see: *Longley, P.A. Singleton, A.D. London Output Area Classification (LOAC) Census Information Scheme, GLA Intelligence, London.*

Life and Death (82-3)

ONS predicts London's population will reach 9 million by 2021: *www.ons.gov.uk/ons/rel/snpp/ sub-national-population-projec- tions/2012-based-projections/stb- 2012-based-snpp.html*

Professional Networking (86-7)

For a full list of the occupation types collected by the 2011 Census, see here: *www.nomisweb. co.uk/census/2011/ys606ew*

High Streets (88-9)

London's high streets are a priority for the GLA. Through Design for London, they funded Gort Scott to undertake the study used here: *www.gortscott.com/project/ high-street-london.* For more infor-mation on the GLA's most recent initiatives, see: *www.london.gov.uk/ priorities/regeneration/high-streets*

There's a Guild for That (90-91)

The colours and dates of London's livery companies were cross-referenced between John Kennedy Melling's *Discovering London's Guilds and Liveries* (Oxford: Shire Publications, 2003) and *The London Encyclopedia* (Weinreb, Hibbert, Keay, Keay. London: Macmillan, 2008). More informa-tion on the individual companies can be found via *liverycompanies. com* or the City of London: *www. cityoflondon.gov.uk/about-the-city/ working-with-and-for-others/Pag- es/city-livery-companies.aspx*

Moving In, Then On (94-5)

Research by the estate agency, Hamptons International, suggests that most moves out of London are around 26 miles. *www.hamp- tons.co.uk/news-research/press- releases/dec-02-2013*

The migration statistics were drawn from the ONS's Statistical Bulletin entitled *Internal Migration by Local Authorities in England and Wales, Year Ending June 2012* (published June 2013).

Increasingly Eastern (96-7) Passports, Please (98-9)

The data and analysis for both of these graphics were derived from a series of 'Census snapshots' published by the GLA: *Diversity in London; Passports held; Country of birth, Passports held and National Identity* – all of which are downloadable from the London Datastore: *data.london.gov.uk*

Page 5 of *Passports held* notes that 7.5 million Londoners held 7.8

million passports because some people held two or more. Tallies of passports count people twice, which is why we used tallies of passport *holders* for our graphics.

EthniCity (100-101)

London's waves of migrants feature in almost every history of the capital. We took our contextual information for this graphic from *London: The Illus trated History* (London: Penguin, 2008) for this graphic.

Greetings from London (104-5)

The statistic that over 300 languages are spoken in London is widely quoted. The original source may be the book *Multilingual Capital* (Philip Baker, John Everseley. London: Battle-bridge Publications, 2000).

Who London Inspired (108-9)

For the most comprehensive guide to London's Blue Plaques, see *Lived in London: Blue Plaques and the Stories Behind Them* (Emily Cole. London: Yale University Press, 2009).

We excerpted Van Gogh's quotes from *The Letters of Vincent Van Gogh* (Mark Roskill, ed. New York: Antheneum, 1963).

WHERE WE GO

There is order and beauty in the chaos of your commute (114-5)

TfL log around 24 million journeys a day across the network: *www.tfl. gov.uk/corporate/about-tfl/what- we-do?intcmp=2582* and release a business plan each year detailing their future plans and how they are seeking to squeeze more capacity from their infrastructure: *www.tfl.gov.uk/cdn/static/cms/ documents/tfl-business-plan-de- cember-2013.pdf*

Untangled on Arrival (116-9)

Wikipedia has a good article on wake turbulence from aircraft: *en.wikipedia.org/wiki/Wake_tur- bulence* and NATS have produced an infographic that explains the need for stacking at Heathrow and other large airports: *nats.aero/ blog/2013/06/infographic-why-do- aircraft-hold-at-heathrow-airport*

The quote 'It's about Britain's place in the world' appears on p. 3 of Heathrow Airport's report entitled *A New Approach*: *www. heathrowairport.com/static/ Heathrow/Downloads/PDF/a-new- approach_LHR.pdf*

Thames Gateway (120-123)

The headline statistics for the Port of London Authority are taken from here: *www.pla.co.uk/assets/ infographicplaporttrade-standard- quality-0.5mb.pdf*

The 'River Thames Whale' has its own Wikipedia entry: *en.wikipe- dia.org/wiki/River_Thames_whale*

The full quote from John Burns is 'The St Lawrence is water, the Mississippi is muddy water, but the Thames is liquid history'. *Daily Mail* (25 January 1943)

Fiona Rule's *London's Docklands: A History of the Lost Quarter* (London: Ian Allen, 2009) offers detailed insights into the origins and history of the docks that provide important context to the area we know today.

For a more detailed history of many key landmarks along the Thames, we recommend the final section (pp. 401-47) of Peter Ackroyd's *Thames Sacred River* (London: Vintage, 2007), from which we drew information for our captions on Isle of Dogs and Hope Reach.

The first chapter of Terry Farrell's book, *Shaping London*, (Chichester: Wiley, 2010) explains how the Thames influenced the development of the capital and provided some useful context to this graphic.

Getting to Work (124-5)

TfL quote 2.4 billion bus journeys in 2013/14 here: *www.tfl.gov.uk/in- fo-for/media/press-releases/2014/ may/annual-passenger-journeys-on- london-s-buses-top-2-4-billion*

For bus fares, see: *www.tfl.gov. uk/fares-and-payments/fares/bus- and-tram*

The 2010 *Future of London Buses* report details the importance of buses as affordable transport: *www.london.gov.uk/sites/default/ files/buses-future.pdf*

To and Fro, on the Tube (126-7)

Page 937 of *The London Encyclopedia* (Weinreb, Hibbert, Keay, Keay. London: Macmillan, 2008) offers a good overview of the conception and creation of London's railways both above and below ground.

The population of the Victorian world was taken from here: *www. un.org/esa/population/publica-tions/sixbillion/sixbilpart1.pdf*

A Week on the Underground (128-9)

The Tube ridership record was broken on 2 August 2012 with 4.32 million journeys: *www.tfl.gov.uk/in-fo-for/media/press-releases/2012/august/london-2012-games-bring-busiest-days-in-tubes-history*

Around the World in 10 Lines (130-131)

Data in this graphic came from the *London Underground Performance Almanac*, which is updated each month: *www.tfl.gov.uk/corporate/publications-and-reports*

Disrupted (132-3)

We obtained the statistics on delays and suicides through two Freedom of Information Requests to TfL: *www.whatdotheyknow.com/request/causes_of_delays_london_undergro* and *www.whatdotheyknow.com/request/suicide_statistics_13*

The changeover time of 218 seconds for Victoria Line drivers is quoted from this article: *www.therailengineer.com/2013/05/08/squeezing-more-from-the-tube*

A summary of the transport improvements implemented in the run up to the 2012 Olympics is outlined in the House of Commons Standard Note SN3722 entitled *London Olympics 2012: Transport.* For more on the legacy of this, see the London Assembly's report entitled *London 2012 and the Transport Legacy* (published February 2013).

The Tube Challenge (134-5)

The rules of the Tube Challenge can be found here: *www.tubefo-rum.co.uk/rules.html*

For more on *Labyrinth,* Art on the Underground's collaboration with artist Mark Wallinger, see here: *art.tfl.gov.uk/labyrinth*

Mental Maps (138-141)

We obtained our 'Knowledge' runs from 'blue books' issued by Taxi Trade Promotions in Spring 2014: *www.taxitradepromotions.co.uk.*

The first study to identify larger hippocampi in taxi drivers was published in 2000: *Maguire, E., Gadian, D., Johnsrude, I., Good, C., Ashburner, J., Frackowiak, R. and Frith, C. 2000. Navigation-related structural change in the hippocampi of taxi drivers. PNAS. 97, 8: 4398-4403.*

Minicab Corridors (142-3)

For the full methodology behind Ed's community detection see: *Manley, E. 2014. Identifying functional urban regions within traffic flow. Regional Studies, Regional Science. 1, 1: 40-42.*

Lost & Found (144-5)

We gathered the data for lost property at Heathrow Airport through a search on *missingx.com* for 1 January to 31 December 2013. For simplicity, some categories on the site were combined.

We obtained statistics from TfL on the number of returned items using a Freedom of Information Request: *www.whatdotheyknow.com/request/lost_property_returns*

The Morning Ride (146-7)

Cycling to work increased 155% in London between the 2001 and 2011 Censuses. Reasons for such an increase were reported by *The Times: www.thetimes.co.uk/tto/public/cyclesafety/article3706006.ece*

There is no guarantee that all the 'Cycle Superhighways' proposed and shown in the graphic will ever be built. For the latest information, see here: *www.tfl.gov.uk/modes/cycling/routes-and-maps/barclays-cycle-superhighways*

Exhausting Rides (150-151)

For the EU recommendation on air pollution limits, we consulted Directive 2008/50/EC of the European Parliament and of the Council of 21 May 2008 on ambient air quality and cleaner air for Europe. *www.euro.who.int/__data/assets/pdf_file/0020/182432/e96762-final.pdf?ua=1*

Our source for estimates of air pollution deaths is the Public Health England report published in 2014 entitled *Estimating Local Mortality Burdens Associated with Particulate Air Pollution: www.hpa.org.uk/webc/HPAwebFile/HPAweb_C/1317141074607*

Cycling is still one of the healthiest ways of getting around the capital as this article in the *British Medical Journal* shows: *www.bmj.com/content/348/bmj.g425*

Cable Car to Nowhere (152-3)

The data for this graphic were found in two existing Freedom of Information Requests: *www.whatdotheyknow.com/request/emirates_air_line_user_figures* and *www.whatdotheyknow.com/request/emirates_air_line_user_numbers*

There has been a steady stream of negative headlines about the Emirates Air Line. Boris Johnson's latest (at the time of writing) attempt to defend it involved hosting his monthly radio phone-in show from one of the gondolas: *www.itv.com/news/london/2014-07-01/boris-insists-underused-cable-car-is-a-howling-success*

Why Not Walk It? (158-9)

The Mark Mason quote is taken from page 4 of his excellent book *Walk the Lines* (London: Random House, 2011).

Tube journey times are taken from TfL's journey planner: *journeyplanner.tfl.gov.uk*

HOW WE'RE DOING

Islington Has Issues (162-3)

The data used in this graphic were taken from the ONS's Statistical Bulletin *Personal Well-Being Across the UK, 2012/13.* The statistics themselves remain experimental, which means they will be tweaked in the future before reaching the gold standards of national statistics such as the census.

It was the best of times, it was the worst of times (164-165)

Written by Charles Dickens, *A Tale of Two Cities* was published in 1859 and is set in both London and Paris.

For more on the recent trends and changes in the distribution of poverty in London, see the report entitled *London's Poverty Profile 2013* published by Trust for London and New Policy Institute.

We quote John Snow from his 1854 report entitled *The Cholera Near Golden Square and at Deptford* in the *Medical Times Gazette.* 9: 321-322.

Lives on the Line (166-7)

For details on how this graphic was created, see this research paper: *Cheshire, J. 2012. Lives on the Line: Mapping Life Expectancy Along the London Tube Network. Environment and Planning A. 44 (7)*

The London Health Observatory first used the Jubilee Line to chart life expectancy. The diagram they used to do it can be found here: *www.lho.org.uk/LHO_Topics/National_Lead_Areas/HealthInequalitiesOverview.aspx*

The 32 Stops (Danny Dorling, London: Penguin, 2013) takes each station along the Central Line and details the social inequalities between those living around them.

The Shape of Obesity (170-171)

For more information on studies of childhood obesity, see Public Heath England's National Child Measurement Programme: *www.gov.uk/government/news/latest-phe-national-child-measure-ment-programme-figures-available*

The GLA Intelligence Unit also published a report in 2011 entitled *Childhood Obesity in London: www.london.gov.uk/sites/default/files/glae-childhood-obesity.pdf*

Causes of Death (172-3)

ONS released these rankings at the request of Clean Air in London: *cleanairinlondon.org/hot-topics/first-ever-rankings-of-top-10-death-rates-for-every-london-borough*

The information on John Graunt comes from Edward Tufte's *The Cognitive Style of PowerPoint* (Graphics Press, 2004) and the *Oxford Dictionary of National Biography: www.oxforddnb.com/view/article/11306*

Quit Dates (174-5)

For more on Stoptober, see Public Health England's press release: *www.gov.uk/government/news/stoptober-challenge-reaches-new-high-as-countrys-biggest-mass-quit-attempt*

Scientific American has a link to the science behind Monday quit days: *www.scientificamerican.com/podcast/episode/mondays-top-quit-smoking-google-sea-13-11-12*

To make this photoillustration, we combined four stock images by photographer Dmitry Maslov.

Pill Boxes (176-7)

The prescription data were a major open data release and one that identified millions of pounds of potential savings for the NHS. *www.economist.com/news/britain/21567980-how-scrutiny-freely-available-data-might-save-nhs-money-beggar-thy-neighbour*

Call 999 (178-9)

For a history of 999 – which first launched in London – see here: *www.bbc.co.uk/news/magazine-18520121*

The £3.5 billion cost statistic comes from Public Health England's October 2013 report, *Alcohol Treatment in England 2012-13: www.nta.nhs.uk/uploads/alcohol2012-13.pdf*

For more on booze buses: *www.londonambulance.nhs.uk/news/alcohol-related_999_incidents.aspx*

Top Crimes (182-3)

'54% of Newham residents' refers to Question 13 from the September 2013 MPS Public Attitude Survey: 'To what extent are you worried about crime in this area?'

You Can't Hide (184-5)

We obtained these flight data through an FOI request: *www.whatdotheyknow.com/request/3_months_of_mps_asu_flight_logs*

To view their photos, follow @MPSinthesky on Twitter. To see videos of their thermal camera in action, check out *content.met.police.uk/Site/airsupportunit*

Sound the Alarm! (186-7)

The #fiftyshadesofred campaign data came from correspondence with the London Fire Brigade as well as their 29 July 2013 press release entitled *Number of people trapped in objects like handcuffs and toilet seat rises: www.london-fire.gov.uk/news/C92C30A17C5547278C728EF-4B9A8B530_2807201320.asp#.U9hU3lBdUZA*

Safer Drivers (188-9)

For more detailed analysis of road safety trends in London, see TfL and the Mayor of London's *Safe Streets for London – London's Road Safety Plan 2012* report published in 2013: *www.tfl.gov.uk/cdn/static/cms/documents/safe-streets-for-london.pdf*

The results from Operation Safeway were reported in *Cycling Weekly. www.cyclingweekly.co.uk/news/latest-news/over-14000-penalised-by-police-in-london-road-safety-operation-19177*

How Cyclists Get Hit (190-191)

This graphic is an adapted version of the diagrams included in a September 2011 Transport for London Surface Transport report entitled *Pedal cyclist collisions and casualties in Greater London.* It also draws from the *Safe Streets for London* action plan: *www.tfl.gov.uk/cdn/static/cms/documents/safe-streets-for-london.pdf*

The ban on unsafe lorries is reported here: *www.theguardian.com/uk-news/2014/jan/30/unsafe-lorry-ban-cyclists-london-m25*

Street Views (192-3)

Data for this graphic were taken from the 2013/14 CHAIN Annual Report: *www.broadwaylondon.org/CHAIN/Reports/S2h2014/S2H%20full_2013-14%20final.pdf*

The Unconnected (194-5)

Data for this graphic come from responses to a question in the 2013 Labour Force Survey: 'When did you last use the Internet?' *data.london.gov.uk/datastore/package/internet-use-borough-and-population-sub-groups*

Top of the Class (196-7)

The quote 'perhaps the biggest question in education policy' is from Sam Freedman, Director of Research, Evaluation and Impact at the education charity Teach First: *samfreedman1.blogspot.co.uk/2014/06/the-london-schools-effect-what-have-we_28.html*

The Institute for Fiscal Studies report cited was published in June 2014 and entitled *Lessons from London Schools for Attainment Gaps and Social Mobility: www.gov.uk/government/uploads/system/uploads/attachment_data/file/321969/London_Schools_-_FINAL.pdf*

CfBT Education Trust's *Lessons from London Schools* was published the same week as the above: *cdn.cfbt.com/~/media/cfbtcorporate/files/research/2014/r-london-schools-2014.pdf*

The BBC's education correspondant, Sean Coughlan, wrote a comprehensive review of both reports here: *www.bbc.co.uk/news/education-28003851*

In Their Words (198-199)

We scraped the word counts for this graphic from nine Ministry of Stories publications: *Green Wobbly Things, Dancing* (2011); *Plenty of Petrol for 106 Miles* (2011); all four volumes of *The Awfully Bad Guide to Monster Housekeeping* (2011); *Detective Flatley's Mysterious and Monstrous Map of Hoxton* (2012); *A Story You Never Tasted Before* (2013); and *Share More Air* (2013).

WHAT WE LIKE

The Football Tribes (202-3)

We used the 'official' hashtags of the football clubs. Chelsea's, for example, is #cfc and #chelseafc.

You and your interests are the future of Big Data (204-5)

The graphic takes data from the *World Cities Culture Report* published in 2013 by the Mayor of London: *www.london.gov.uk/sites/default/files/WCCR2013.pdf*

The BBC reported on the smart bins: *www.bbc.co.uk/news/technology-23665490*

The Alex Deane quote comes from his post on Big Brother Watch: *www.bigbrotherwatch.org.uk/home/2013/08/bin-snooping-weve-been-here-before.html*

A True Zoo (201-11)

Press releases about the tigers and Partula snails were found on ZSL's website: *www.zsl.org*

'374,000 living animals' refers to ISIS's Zoological Information Management System (ZIMS): *www2.isis.org/products/Pages/default.aspx*

All the Tate's Treasures (212-3)

The Tate Collection make it easy to download all their catalogue data from here: *github.com/tategallery/collection*

Following the Leader (214-5)

An earlier version of this graphic originally appeared in *IL Magazine #14* in November 2009. We updated it to include wheels that have been built since then.

For reference, we consulted photographs, the Observation Wheel Directory *www.observation-wheeldirectory.com* and Wikipedia: *en.wikipedia.org/wiki/List_of_Ferris_wheels*

Fashion Cycles (216-7)

Each season, EDITD offers 'Digital Trend Reviews' from the four fashion weeks: *editd.com/resources*

They Came, They Saw, They Spent (218-9)

The ONS calculates passenger spending using their International Passenger Survey: *www.ons.gov.uk/ons/guide-method/method-quality/specific/travel-and-transport-methodology/international-passenger-survey/index.html*

The 2013 visitor numbers came from here: *www.ons.gov.uk/ons/rel/ott/travel-trends/2013/sty.html*

GLA Economics published a working paper in 2012 (#53) entitled *Tourism in London* that details the growth in visitor numbers and how much they spend: *www.london.gov.uk/sites/default/files/wp53.pdf*

Who Says Print is Dead? (222-3)

We measured the newspapers as they were stacked in their stands and made back-of-the-envelope calculations to establish their approximate thickness.

Our circulation figures come from Wikipedia: *en.wikipedia.org/wiki/List_of_newspapers_in_the_United_Kingdom_by_circulation*

Looking for Love (226-7)

Headline results from the ONS's *2012 Integrated Household Survey* are available here: *www.ons.gov.uk/ons/rel/integrated-household-survey/integrated-household-survey/january-to-december-2012/info-sexual-identity.html?WT.mc_id=74d8bdd269c255d-06715cf7e3ff9352c&WT.z_taxonomy=pop&WT.z_format=draws%20you%20in&WT.z_content=interactive&WT.z_trigger=proactive*

Happy Times (228-9)

For more about *Mappiness*, watch an interview with George MacKerron: *www.theguardian.com/technology/2011/feb/13/bright-idea-mappiness-happiness-app* or visit: *www.mappiness.org.uk*

Journalist Olaf Storbeck keeps a tally of severe cyclist crashes in this Google Doc: *docs.google.com/spreadsheet/ccc?key=0AuEt-gCUuVBDUdHZqbEZ1NVctVTBVe-FRqTmNVbGZnbXc&hl=de#gid=0*